No Longer Forgotten

Incredible Stories of Faith, Hope and Resilience

Advantage™
INSPIRATIONAL

Stanley M. Mutunga

NO LONGER FORGOTTEN
Incredible Stories of Faith, Hope and Resilience
by Stanley Mutunga

Copyright © 2010 by Stanley M. Mutunga
All Rights Reserved
ISBN: 1-59755-251-8
ISBN 13: 978-1-59755-251-6

Published by: ADVANTAGE BOOKS™
www.advbookstore.com

Scripture quotations marked NLT are taken from the Holy Bible, New Living Translation, copyright 1996, 2004. Used by permission of Tyndale House Publishers, Inc., Wheaton, Illinois 60189. All rights reserved.

Library of Congress Control Number:

First Printing June 2010
10 11 12 13 14 15 16   10 9 8 7 6 5 4 3 2 1
Printed in the United States of America

DEDICATION

First, I want to dedicate this book to my late parents, Peter and Grace, for introducing me to Christ and instilling in me the virtues of respect for others, godly humility and service to those in need.

I also dedicate it to my wife Rose and our three sons Jason, James and Jack who have been with me on this journey of serving God through others. Their encouragement and patience with me have been invaluable throughout the journey.

Last but not the least, I want to dedicate this book to the many AIDS orphans, widows and their families who over the years have patiently taught me many lessons of life that I could not have otherwise learned. Hopefully, I am a better human being as a result of their incredible faith, hope in God and uncommon resilience.

Stanley M. Mutunga

What people are saying about

No Longer Forgotten

No Longer Forgotten is not written from the confines of a cozy study in the USA, Dr. Mutunga writes from the perspective of an African. He was born and raised in southeastern Kenya and understands the culture and how to provide an effective "hand up" to those who have been left hopeless in the wake of HIV/AIDS. Each chapter contains moving stories of real people who have been helped by one of three different organizations that are serving orphaned children and adults.

Biblical concepts are coupled with readable analysis, statistics and important insights on responding to the needs of Africa in general and specifically in Kenya. The book will provide encouragement for the involvement of churches and individuals in bringing new hope and new life to those suffering the consequences of arguably the most devastating human disaster in modern times. A must read for pastors, missions committees, and anyone interested in seeing God's grace and mercy applied in tender and effective ways.

Dr. Roger Beard
Lead Pastor (Retired), Parkcrest Christian Church, Long Beach California

****

It was a sad day for me when Stanley Mutunga came to my office to resign as Hope International University's Dean of the School of Graduate Studies. He would continue to teach for us, he explained, but he needed his summers and other break times to take care of HIV/AIDS orphans in his home country of Kenya. That was in 2002. Since then Tumaini, the rescue operation he founded, has given hope to over a thousand AIDS-orphaned children. Obviously the Dean made the right decision.

No Longer Forgotten recounts the results of Dr. Mutunga's selfless decision. Having seen Tumaini's ministry up close and personal, I can attest to the book's authenticity. I think you, too, will be moved by the testimonies, instructed by the research, impressed by the strategy, and inspired to find your own means of giving hope to otherwise forgotten people.

Dr. LeRoy Lawson
Former President, Hope International University, International Consultant, CMF International, Indianapolis Indiana

****

In the age of the "me first" mentality, *No Longer Forgotten* sounds the call for corporate connectedness. As Christians, we are all part of the family of God, and are biblically mandated to reach out to others. Dr. Mutunga illustrates that when people of different cultures, tribes and nations actually *do* come together under the banner of Christ, we witness the hand of God at work not only in the lives of those we seek to touch, but in our own lives as well. Whether you are serving as a pastor, church leader, or simply as a follower of Jesus, this book will challenge you to think beyond what you believe possible and sense this call to connectedness in your own life and ministry.

Mike Spradlin
Lead Pastor, Valley Christian Church, Chino California

ACKNOWLEDGMENTS

Thank you ……..

Dr. Doug McConnell, my friend and Dean of the School of Intercultural Studies at Fuller Theological Seminary for the many hours you put into this work. In your Forward, you actually managed to better articulate some of what I tried to say in many pages in the book! Thank you brother!

Dr. LeRoy Lawson, my dear friend and former President of Hope International University. Your pastoral, academic and international experience in church work and on the matters raised in this book made your comments invaluable as I labored through the write up.

Dr. Roger Beard, my colleague in ministry and a dear friend. Your humility, passion and dedication to those affected and infected with the AIDS scourge in Africa is simply unmatched. The experiences you shared with me of your 38 years of ministry as a senior pastor was incredibly helpful to me and I so much valued it as I completed this book.

Pastor Mike Spradlin, my friend and partner in ministry for your constructive criticism and encouragement meant so much to me. Your enthusiasm for this work and engaging comments were incredibly helpful. What a mind God has given you!

Michelle Lewis, my long time friend and partner in ministry. "Thank you" is simply not enough but that is all I will say! Thank you for taking your countless hours to read my tedious drafts of this book and patiently make it readable.

To all my ministry partners in the USA and Africa. So many of you offered suggestions and encouragement along the way. I am eternally grateful to all of you.

Table of Contents

Stanley M. Mutunga

FOREWORD

Listening to the latest reports on the HIV/AIDS pandemic leave us with an overwhelming sense of hopelessness. Millions of orphans, children heading households, and grandparents facing the prospects of raising yet another generation on meager resources are realities for far too many of our fellow human beings on this planet. Attempts to reduce the spread are fraught with challenges, not the least of which is the unreliability of systems in place to distribute relief. To be sure, there is an army of people working on making a difference; some like Bill Gates and Bono, bring considerable resources to the task. But by any standard, the scale of this battle is beyond any single group, however broad their resource base. As one student observed, it is truly a "God-sized problem."

One encouraging front in the battle against HIV/AIDS is the response of churches, both in areas devastated by the disease and those in parts of the world where the impact is less readily observed. Local efforts to make a difference in Africa were the surprising finding of a major study of six countries on the continent.[1] Churches in other parts of the world are responding in ways that are both helpful and in some cases, not so helpful. The critical question for churches and Christian leaders today is not if, but how we should be involved in this long-term battle against the pandemic.

Dr. Stanley Mutunga, pastor, teacher, scholar, and missionary, provides a most helpful introduction to the scope of the problems clothed in the lives of the victims and those who are discovering the joy of reaching out in love. As a scholar-practitioner, Dr. Mutunga combines the stories of real people with the deeper issues surrounding this terrible disease. As a Kenyan, his heart for his people comes through loud and clear. Each chapter introduces cases of individuals who have turned from victims into not only survivors, but in many instances into those who are bringing help to the afflicted. True to his international perspective, Dr.

Mutunga relates the joy that comes to those who leave the comforts of home to share in the lives of those in more desperate situations.

Mutunga does not shy away from the toughest issues that frame the context of the pandemic. Reading his treatment of political corruption, for example, leaves one with a sense that wide scale positive change is impossible. One response could be to refuse to respond. But just as the reader wants to turn away, Mutunga draws on a parable from India contexting it in our Christian response. "Corruption" he writes, "and all manner of social evils should not change the Christians' nature to want to help the poor and the downtrodden." This includes a variety of problems, the most virulent of all being poverty in all its insidious dimensions.

An important consideration, clearly treated by Dr. Mutunga, is the area of relationships, foundational to both the nature and the sustainability of our response. Contrasting the worldviews of Kenyans and Westerners, he draws on the biblical notion of the family of God, to help us understand the inclusive nature of our being.

> *The people of God, wherever they may be found belong to the same family. We are wa kwetu.[2] If we truly belong to the family of God, then the non-poor cannot simply sit and enjoy life while part of the family is perishing in inhumane conditions. Wa kwetu calls us to remember that we are our brothers and sisters keeper wherever the brother and sister may be found on the globe.*

The book continues to develop the themes of Christian responses through partnerships by providing examples of responses from his organization, Tumaini International Ministries, as well as others. Thankfully, Dr. Mutunga's treatment of the elements of a Christian response includes the need to multiply the presence and response of churches, central to the mission of God in our time. In true missionary form, he combines passion and practicalities for the reader, leaving us ready to respond in tangible ways.

Dr. Mutunga helps us to embrace the importance of our god-given memory, individually and collectively. Even the title, No Longer

Forgotten, is a message of resistance against apathy. As a fellow alumnus of Fuller Seminary, a friend, and a colleague of Stanley Mutunga, I commend this book to you as an important part of a genuine response to HIV/AIDS, one of the most deadly of the 21st century pandemics.

Douglas McConnell
Dean, School of Intercultural Studies
Fuller Theological Seminary

Stanley M. Mutunga

PREFACE

The friend who can be silent with us in a moment of despair and confusion, who can stay with us in the hour of grief and bereavement, who can tolerate not-knowing, not curing, not healing, and face with us the reality of our powerlessness, that is the friend who cares. **Henri J M Nouwen,** *The Dance of Life: Weaving Sorrows And Blessings into One Joyful Step*

October, 2000: I knew something had gone terribly wrong. I had been out of Kenya for a few years, and was back to bury a brother. Everywhere, there were casket shops. I don't know why I noticed it more this time but I saw many outdoor shops making caskets, in both small and big towns. Furthermore, I noticed in the villages that they were burying their loved ones every day! When I was growing up, burials were typically done only on Saturdays. Not anymore! This time around, there were burial ceremonies on Mondays, Tuesdays, Wednesdays, Thursdays, Fridays and yes of course, on Saturdays. There were burials on Sundays too.

What had changed? Well, in those days, AIDS was reportedly killing some 700 people every day in Kenya. Grandparents were forced to get busy burying their sons and daughters and becoming parents all over again. Older siblings were missing school to take care of their dying parents. Some were assuming parental responsibilities to help their tired grandparents. The grandparents were suffering a double jeopardy by losing their sons and daughters as well as economic sustenance. The picture was bleak.

In many ways, this book traces its genesis from that initial experience back in October 2000. I am writing out of personal experience with the HIV/AIDS pandemic. Like many people, prior to this experience, I had read about the disease for many years since it was first given a name in the early 1980s. But when I began to lose family members, my eyes began to open to the anguish and suffering that the disease was leaving on its destructive path. I knew then that I needed to do something about the situation. I sensed God's call not only to me, but also to the Church. I heard God challenging me personally and urging me to call the Church from her slumber and be a good neighbor to the millions of AIDS orphans and their families.

At the time I was Dean of the Graduate School at Hope International University in Fullerton, California. My trips to Kenya became more frequent and the Lord kept nudging my heart to seek ways to assist children who had been otherwise forgotten by the larger society. Something that I had noticed in my visit in 2000 kept bothering my heart. Poor grandparents and the community at large were too busy burying their dead and no one seriously paid close attention to the plight of the millions of orphans who were being left behind. Orphans as young as eight years old were helping to care for their dying parents, and these children were quickly becoming "parents" to their younger siblings.

In the spring of 2003, I tendered my resignation as Dean and transitioned to a nine-month professorship commitment so that I could begin to do something about the AIDS scourge in Kenya. At that time it was widely believed that only 3% of U.S churches were responding to AIDS in some fashion, either because the majority of Christians were wholly unaware of the devastation being caused by this unforgiving disease, or, perhaps worse, those who did know felt that "those people should know better." The more I got involved, the more I saw that the AIDS orphans and the poor grandparents, who were taking care of them, particularly in sub-Saharan Africa, were a forgotten lot. I felt the Lord calling me to respond in some tangible way, and that is when I founded **Tumaini International Ministries** as a conduit to garner support from friends and Christians in the U.S and Kenya to assist these children. *Tumaini* is the Kiswahili word for *hope.* My vision was very clear. I wanted to connect ministers and ordinary Christians in the U.S. with those forgotten families in Kenya and beyond. I wanted to start an outreach where participants would feel empowered, and create a sustainable ministry where both the sponsor and the recipient would learn from each other and develop a mutual relationship through Vision Trips and regular correspondence.

However, I recognized very early on that this needed to be more than a typical child sponsorship program. Rather, what was needed was long-term commitment to help the kids grow without necessarily creating a dependency syndrome. This meant that kids would not only be helped for a few years to earn their high school diplomas, but also assisted to learn a trade or go to college. I recognized that rather than creating orphanages I would use the existing social systems of extended family care. Even where both parents had died, I knew that the orphans could still live with relatives, family friends or caring neighbors.

Collaboration with Other Agencies

What was even more exciting for me was to find other grassroots Christian agencies that were attempting to address the same issues, especially in the urban slums. As I look back now, I believe that we have been able to learn from and network with these organizations and collectively we are all stronger in our respective ministries. Specifically, it has been an honor to learn from two such organizations: Health Education for Africa Resource Teams (HEART) and Community Transformers. These agencies have impacted the lives of thousands of AIDS orphans and widows in the slums of Kibera and Mathare in the City of Nairobi and I have cited a few cases from their work.

Over the past six years, I have spent countless hours listening to many, many sad stories of the orphans. I have listened to HIV-positive widows, some of them on their dying beds, begging the world not to forget their children when they are gone. I have also met some wonderful Christians from Kenya and America who have come alongside to journey with these forgotten brothers and sisters and to offer a hands-up as they face uncertain futures. This book is replete with such stories. Stories of desperation. Stories of hope. Stories of resilience and determination. Stories of hope bearers. Stories of incredible networking and partnerships that only God in His unfathomable providence can make possible.

No Longer Forgotten is therefore a collection of incredible stories of hope and resilience. The book is a testimony of what God can do in and through broken vessels such as us to bring hope to thousands of otherwise forgotten AIDS orphans, widows and their families. Except for Muli in Chapter One, the names of the children and their families have been changed- but the stories are as real and devastating as presented.

Book Outlay

In Part I, I *set the stage* by introducing the readers to a boy named Muli (pronounced "Moo-lee") and his grandmother Ndunge (pronounced "Doon-gay"). Muli, an AIDS orphan, and his grandmother find themselves in a socio-economic, emotional and spiritual state that is representative of millions of families in sub-Saharan Africa as a result of the AIDS scourge that has ravaged the region. Their personal story and how it unfolds is a microcosm of the stories of many such families. As the story unfolds, what is key is the difference that the church of Jesus Christ makes in this family. It is an example of the difference that ordinary Christians can bring to a suffering family in Africa and other similar contexts. It is a story of hope which ordinary Christians can bring to millions of vulnerable and orphaned children all over the world.

In Part II, I narrow the discussion to a *socio-economic context*. Sharing real-life stories of families who have been negatively impacted from the decimation of wage earners by the unforgiving AIDS disease, I highlight on both the micro- and macroeconomic factors affecting Africa vis-à-vis the rest of the world. I explain why the poor find themselves in the current situation of utter poverty, pointing to both the broken walls of local and international politics as well as the national calamities. I propose that the church of Jesus Christ has no luxury of asking whether it should get involved or not. The resounding answer is yes and the only question is how. This leads to the need for a well formulated missional approach that recognizes the need and draws both its methodology and impetus from Jesus Christ himself.

In Part III, I delve deeper into the issue of *missional context*. Specifically, I discuss the salient areas of ministry needs in dealing with AIDS orphans or children at risk in general. I take a fresh look at some key aspects of holistic ministry—spiritual, social, physical and emotional. I argue that in ministering to the AIDS orphans, the church of Jesus Christ must take a longitudinal approach. These are kids who have lost everything—parents, the only providers and role models in their lives and consequently their hope. It then becomes critically important to minister to their whole needs.

In Part IV, I focus on *strategic partnerships*. Given the needs, I ask such questions as, 'how is the church of Jesus Christ to minister to the millions who form this forgotten but beloved segment of the society?' I highlight the partnerships that Tumaini, HEART and Community Transformers have forged with believers from across the globe. In this age of information technology, global village, and flat world, it is easier than at any other time since William Carey's inaugural world mission to India in 1792. Today, it is technologically easier to work together and make a difference anywhere around the globe in real time.

In Part V, I conclude the book by focusing on *future partnerships*. I provide examples or areas of ministry where churches and mission agencies can partner together for a greater good. Here I cite key biblical passages where the church of Jesus Christ is called to show mercy and compassion instead of empty fasting. The church of Jesus Christ is called to love God and neighbor, pointing out that the children under discussion are the neighbors that God has put in our day to minister to. The Church cannot look the other way and ignore millions of children. Our response, however, should not be out of guilt but out of love for God.

December 15th, 2009. Riverside, California, USA.
smmutunga@hotmail.com
smutunga@sbcglobal.net

Stanley M. Mutunga

Chapter 1

"My Name is Muli"

When we pulled into their compound, the shy little boy was holding tightly to his grandmother's arms. He was hesitant to shake hands with strangers. This was understandable because he had never met white people before, let alone having them come to his humble home. His grandmother urged him to come forward and greet the guests. After much persuasion and with one hand covering his face, the little boy outstretched his right hand and shook hands with all the nine guests who had just swarmed his home. Meanwhile, the neighbors were quickly and curiously gathering around to find out who the strangers were and why they could possibly be visiting such a humble home. As is often the case, the neighbors quickly brought in enough 'chairs' for the guests, a sign of spontaneous hospitality one witnesses in much of sub-Saharan Africa.

"What is your name?" I asked the young boy. "Muli", he said and quickly retreated to his quiet and respectful posture. I explained to my American friends that the name Muli (pronounced *Moo*-lee) in the local Kikamba language meant "one who has been forgotten." Unbeknown to Muli, things were about to take a dramatic turn for him personally and, indeed, for his family.

Ndunge, the Grandmother

At this point, Ndunge (pronounced *Doon*-gay), the boy's grandmother, had joined in the conversation and told us the unforgettable story about Muli. Muli had lost his father to AIDS when he was barely five years old. When the father died, Muli's mother moved back to her maternal family and 'dropped' the child with Ndunge and headed for the city of Nairobi, never to be seen again. In talking with the family members, no one seemed to know exactly where or how his ailing mother was except that she had left their humble home sickly for the big city. Running away to the anonymity of the big cities is common due to the stigma still associated with HIV and AIDS. Ndunge went on to narrate the sad story of how she had unwittingly joined the ranks of a growing number of grandmothers who are becoming mothers all over again after losing their sons and daughters to the AIDS pandemic.

One of the devastating effects of AIDS is that it has proved to be a double-edged sword. It claims the lives of the young working class, leaving behind both the children and elderly grandparents with little or no means to care for themselves. Since there is no social security system for Ndunge, her situation is worse than that of the average poor person. At age 61 and a widow, Ndunge told us how she had to rely on very meager resources. Only one of her daughters is capable of taking care of her own two children, leaving Ndunge with the responsibility of the others. Subsistence farming is the basic economic sustenance in much of SE Kenya. In Ndunge's case, she has a three-acre plot of land that barely produces enough to feed herself and four of her six grandchildren. That is, when there is enough rain to produce edible crops at all.

As I sat there that morning and listened to Ndunge, I could not help but notice her confident, beaming personality and unfaltering gratefulness to God "for the great things he has done" for her. For me, such a high sense of God's presence and provision belied the stark reality of the abject poverty that was evident everywhere, right before us. It seemed like she was numb to the difficult reality of raising the grandchildren that she so much loves. Yet, she is a woman who sees life through the eyes of faith. During the course of the visit, one of the visitors rightly wondered, *how can Ndunge be so poor and yet so happy?* For those of us used to western abundance, it is humanly impossible to explain her contagious warmth and joy for life against the backdrop of crushing poverty. There is no question that God was teaching me right there and then something about the bigger things in life—not material goods but confidence in the God who truly cares for his children always and everywhere. We had gone to Ndunge's home to encourage her, but I left her home more challenged and encouraged at the same time by her faith in God.

Mike and Hailey

For years, Muli was just one of the millions of forgotten AIDS orphans in Kenya. That was until this one summer morning in August 2007. That morning, something special happened. This was not just for Muli but indeed, the entire village where Muli and Ndunge call their home. What he and his grandmother didn't know was that, on this particular morning, the team from Southern California had purposely visited Muli's home because he had been given a sponsor.

One of the leading partner churches with Tumaini International Ministries was in Kenya on a Vision Trip. This church has made a significant investment in the lives of hundreds of AIDS orphans already in Kenya. In fact, this was the second Vision Trip the lead pastor had taken. Mike, one of the team members, was interested in sponsoring Muli after learning earlier of his needs. What followed was one of the most beautiful experiences of grace to watch as Mike explained to little Muli that Mike's family would from now on provide sponsorship money to allow him to have his basic needs met—school, health care, clothes and food. Mike's teenaged daughter, Hailey, was also on the trip. Both Muli and Ndunge could not hide their joy at the news of his sponsorship. In fact, Muli cried tears of joy as the team set to leave the compound that morning. I will never forget Mike's tearful departing words to Muli: *"You are no longer forgotten."* On that day, Muli had found hope. He had found an extended family more than 8,000 miles away. Moreover, in the same instant, his grandmother Ndunge's hope was renewed.

It has been more than two years since that visit, but the relationship has continued through regular letter writing and photo exchanges. Muli is a bright student, in fact he is usually in position one in his grade level. There is hope for him, not only academically but also spiritually. In a rather unique way, Ndunge, Tumaini, and Mike's family forged a relationship to help raise Muli from that day on.

Visiting with Muli a year later, I was gratified to see the transformation and radiance on the boy's face because of the hope he now has of making it in life. He exudes a level of confidence that was absent when I first met him in the summer 2007. Ndunge is equally a changed woman. She is now used to receiving guests and confident that by working together, her grandson has a bright future. She continues to thank God for using Mike to help in meeting her needs.

No Longer Forgotten

The unfolding success story of Muli and Ndunge illustrates the hope that millions of suffering AIDS orphans in sub-Saharan Africa and beyond can find through caring Christians. Mike's words to Muli that he was *no longer forgotten* registered in my mind in a very special way. This announcement was not just for Muli, but for hundreds of orphans and widows whose lives have been transformed through ministry to this special group of people. It has been an amazing journey to see how through a grassroots approach and minimum bureaucracy, believers are able to network the poor and the non-poor and allow the Lord to minister to both in a mutually beneficial way.

God has laid a burden on my heart to connect ministers and ordinary Christians in the U.S. and Kenya with the needs of forgotten families in Africa. AIDS orphans have lost so much. The direct involvement of Mike and his family in the life of a small boy in SE Kenya illustrates how feasible it is for believers to connect with millions of AIDS orphans and other vulnerable children throughout the world. One of the enduring lessons we are learning through these relationships is that Christians from non-poor nations have something to learn from the poor in Africa. Grandmothers who have nothing in material wealth astound the non-poor with their happy outlook on life and remain responsible in taking care of their grandchildren. I am continually learning that what they really need is a helping hand, not handouts.

Extended Family Care

As I have watched Muli grow over the past two years, my firm belief in keeping orphans with extended family members as opposed to institutional housing has been strengthened. Apart from the fact that it is cheaper, this model is optimal for the children's social and psychological development. Extended family care also makes it possible for the family to continue making a contribution toward the child's support. In Ndunge's case, she is getting a helping hand with some big-ticket items like health care, school expenses and additional food. However, Ndunge still does some chores—such as tilling the ground to supplement the food that the family needs. Above all, she is the one responsible for taking care of the children on daily basis.

A couple years ago, I had a lengthy conversation with a donor who wondered why I could not allow him to send $100 a month instead of $30. He indicated to me on the phone that he knew enough about his sponsored child's family needs and that they could use additional funds. I agreed with him that in a country where the average person lives on under $2.00 a day, it was true that the family can use $100 a month. However, I respectively pointed out to him that as a Christian agency, we were not trying to spoil or break families. Instead, we were only trying to give them a hand-up. You see, good as it sounds, giving a family everything they need deprives them the opportunity to do their part and they become dependent on the freebies. The gentleman finally saw my point.

Although I grew up very poor, God is teaching me afresh that the poor already know how to survive way before I show up. What they need is a hand-up to address some of their acute needs and then empower them to solve their own challenges. Giving Muli access to education, providing for some of his critical healthcare needs and introducing him to the Lord is the best long-term solution to his needs. Allowing Ndunge to participate in raising her grandson will provide Muli with a background of both hardships and blessings that will make him a more complete and compassionate human being.

Good as they can be, orphanages deprive children in Africa an opportunity to grow up in an extended family setting. As I will show in the next few chapters, the extended family model, however imperfect, is still the optimal place to raise the millions of AIDS orphans.

Ndunge's & Muli's Story: Microcosm of a Bigger Story

Ndunge's case is not an isolated one. Indeed, Ndunge's life story is a microcosm of the growing challenge in Kenya and other parts of sub-Saharan Africa due to the impact of HIV and AIDS. Although there are reports indicating that overall HIV infection prevalence in Kenya has declined from 14% in the mid-1990s to 5% in 2006, deaths from those who are already infected, estimated to be about 1 million, will continue to leave thousands of forgotten orphans behind[3]. According to available statistics the number of people dying daily from AIDS complications has dropped from 700 in 1999 to about 300 in 2007. Still these deaths are leaving an estimated 1.6 million orphans in Kenya alone.[4] In addition, with HIV/AIDS affecting the young breadwinners between the ages of 15 and 49, the youth and the elderly are being left without any economic sustenance[5]. The working adults serve as "social security" for their parents and that is lost through this staggering number of deaths. Youth are left economically vulnerable, and they lack parental guidance during crucial, formative years as they swap roles to serve as the caretakers of their dying parents.

These stories tell us only one thing. In the short term, it is only going to get worse. Even though the number of deaths has declined, still the number of orphans left behind will remain significant in the foreseeable future. God is clearly calling his Church to come alongside these children and make life more livable for them.

AIDS Scourge: A Challenge to Socio-Cultural Norms

This state of affairs has caused a heavy burden on grandparents, especially the grandmothers who tend to live longer than their husbands and therefore have the responsibility of raising their orphaned grandchildren. For the first time, some serious challenges are being posed with respect to the basic African worldview of interdependence. Eleven years ago, I wrote a book chapter entitled, *Who Raises a Child When There is No Village?* My context in that write-up was the city. Ministering in the city of Nairobi at the time, I was dealing with street families who had no traditional roots in the city and called the Church to become the extended family. My focus here, however, is the more rural Africa. The question then is, does it still take a village to raise a child in Africa? If that social consciousness is still operational, why do we have so many forgotten AIDS orphans in the villages? Given that the average age of the grandmothers taking care of AIDS orphans is 72 years, who will take care of those orphans when they are gone? Is the African social fabric of extended family falling apart? With the grandmothers gone, are there other functional substitutes that will ensure that kids like Muli have a caring guardian to fall back on until they become adults? Where are the villagers when Ndunge seems to be suffocating in a lonely journey of untold poverty? These and others are important questions that I will revisit later in the book.But now, a quick look at the role of governments in alleviating AIDS pandemic.

Government Responsibility

What is the government of Kenya and other African countries doing to address the needs of its citizens in the face of this unprecedented pandemic? What about the international community? For example, what role are bodies such as the United Nations playing through its many financial aid programs, such as World Bank and International Monitory Fund? There are also other related questions on transparency and accountability. For example, does the money sent to African governments ever actually reach the intended recipients? If it does, why do we still have Muli's and thousands of other similar cases? Are the secular governments and agencies not capable of comprehensively addressing this menacing challenge caused by AIDS?

The Role of the African Church

Turning to the African Church, what is her role and responsibility to these forgotten children and their grandparents? For example, what has Ndunge's church done in response to her felt needs in the face of the HIV/AIDS scourge? What about the Kenyan Christians and churches in general? Have churches done everything in their power to address the needs of these lovely children? Who will come alongside these children and help them realize their God-given dreams and aspirations if the Church stays away from it? Has the Church in Africa taken her ministry to widows and orphans seriously?

The Unfortunate Truth

I will be the first one to admit that in general, the Church in Africa has not done enough to address the HIV/AIDS scourge. Speaking for myself, HIV/AIDS had remained an academic discussion for a good seventeen years before it hit too close to home. It wasn't until I lost family members that I began to get involved in a tangible way. I think C.S. Lewis was correct when he observed that *"God whispers to us in our pleasure, speaks in our conscience, but shouts in our pains: it is his megaphone to rouse a deaf world.*[6] A megaphone is definitely what God had to use on me. No excuse. It's just the plain truth.

Others on the African continent have given many reasons or excuses as to why this has been the case. Some of the reasons are *historical*, such as the idea that giving to missions is a western thing. So there has been the idea that western Christian agencies will tackle the AIDS problem just as they have historically done with other needs and catastrophes.

Still, others hide behind the *moral* code. There are those who feel that AIDS is a disease that is caused by sexual sin and therefore death is the payment for such sins. Others simply remain *ignorant* about the disease. Some in this latter category hold all manner of superstitious beliefs about the cause of the disease, including witch craft. Statements uttered by some African leaders in the recent past did not help in curbing the disease. For example, there was a categorical *denial of* the existence of such a disease by a leader of a key African nation.

The only problem with these and other excuses is that, HIV/AIDS is a reality and does not discriminate. AIDS kills both Christians and non Christians alike. It kills both the rich and the poor alike. It kills people all over the world although 70% of these deaths have occurred in sub-Saharan Africa. As it is commonly said, HIV/AIDS has either affected or infected everyone on the African continent. For whatever reason, in general, Christians in Africa did not proactively address this issue seriously before it got out of hand.

The Church's Call

It seems to me that one of the Church's central callings is to restore *shalom*, the peace and wholeness that was lost as a result of mankind's sin. One of the negative effects of that lost shalom is the existence of diseases such as HIV/AIDS. In bringing about this shalom, I believe that the church community has been called to address at least four main categories of God's people:

1.) *First, the Church is called to reach the lost and bring them to the saving knowledge of Jesus Christ*. God has opened a unique opportunity through the AIDS scourge to share his love with the victims, especially the orphans who have lost the people they love the most, their parents. Too often these children are not only forgotten materially but also spiritually. More than ever before, these orphans need to know the love of God. God's love and call for **all** to come to know him through Jesus Christ is repeated several times in the New Testament. For me, introducing orphans to Christ is central to everything we do. In <u>Matthew 28:18-20,</u> Jesus said, *"...All authority in heaven and on earth has been given to me. Therefore, go and make disciples of all nations baptizing them in the name of the Father and of the Son and of the Holy Spirit, and teaching them to obey everything I have commanded you. And surely I am with you always, to the end of the age." (NIV)*

John 20:21 reads, *"And Jesus said, 'Peace be with you!' As the Father has sent me, I am sending you." (NIV)*

And in Acts 1:8 it says, *"But you will receive power when the Holy Spirit comes on you and you will be my witnesses in Jerusalem, and in all Judea and Samaria, and to the ends of the earth." (NIV)*

I believe that the Church is the vehicle through which this love of God is to be dispensed. God wants to establish an everlasting relationship with these forgotten orphans. God wants to restore something important that AIDS has taken away from them. He wants to restore shalom, once and for all.

2.) *A second key aspect of ministry is in meeting the needs of the poor*. I see poverty as an opportunity for non-poor believers to practice godly stewardship and share their material wealth with those less fortunate. Whatever material wealth we may have as Christians is never about us or for us. We are temporary custodians and guardians of God's wealth. What an opportunity and privilege the Church has to change the course of so many lives. Scripture talks about this responsibility in both the Old and the New Testaments. For example in Deut. 15:11 the Bible says, *"There will always be poor people in the land. Therefore I command you to be openhanded toward your brothers and toward the poor." (NIV)*

In Prov. 19:17, it further states, *"He who is kind to the poor lends to the Lord, and he will reward him for what he has done."* (NIV) God is always calling his church to be generous and there is a blessing that follows.

3.) *Third, ministering to the widows and orphans is critical in both Testaments*. This pair is always mentioned together in the scriptures, as there is a significant element of defenselessness associated with their status. Especially in traditional societies, widows and orphans are a vulnerable group because of the way social laws are set up. It is interesting that the scriptures are equally clear on assisting this vulnerable group.

For example, in <u>Psalm 146</u>:9 it says, *"The Lord watches over the alien and <u>sustains the fatherless and the widow</u>, but he frustrates the ways of the wicked." (NIV, emphasis added).*

In <u>James 1: 27</u> the author says, *"Religion that our Father accepts as pure and faultless is this: to look after orphans and widows in their distress and to keep oneself from being polluted by the world." (NIV)* Again, the opportunities for the Church to affect this group are endless.

4.) Fourth and finally, ministering to the alien is close to God's heart. Regardless of which side of the political divide we find ourselves on the matter of resident aliens, it was important enough for God to remind his people to care for the aliens. For example in <u>Psalm 146:9</u>, the writer says, "The Lord watches over *the alien* and sustains the fatherless and the widow, but he frustrates the ways of the wicked." (NIV, emphasis added). In <u>Ephesians 2:12</u>, Paul says, "Remember that at that time you were separate from Christ, excluded from citizenship in Israel and foreigners to the covenants of the promise, without hope and without God in the world." (NIV) Perhaps as Paul reminded the church at Ephesus, if Christians saw themselves as aliens and foreigners until we met Christ and become sojourners we would better appreciate the place of aliens and foreigners around us.

I see these four general categories of ministry running as key themes throughout the scriptures. God has given the Church endless opportunities to reconcile the forgotten to himself so that they are no longer "foreigners to the covenants of the promise." There are opportunities to meet their physical needs so that their temporal lives can be more bearable. God has blessed the church community to be his feet and hands to put a smile on the faces of these forgotten children.

Working together with extended family members, the Church and other concerned communities can help restore shalom to the affected communities. Muli and his grandmother Ndunge represent not only unique needs and challenges but also opportunities for the Church to bless and be blessed. Ndunge loves her grandchildren but she has a huge responsibility of taking care of them by herself. The rest of us are only coming alongside to give Ndunge a hand so that she can raise her grandchildren. Mike who lives 8000 miles away is only helping Ndunge do her job.

The Way Forward

I am learning that despite the challenges brought about by HIV/AIDS, there is hope as the people of God do their part. When churches, universities, community leaders, extended family members and others work together, God is able to bring shalom to very bleak situations. Millions of forgotten children can be effectively reached with the love of God.

In the chapters that follow, I will share encounters with some orphans, grandmothers, widows, pastors, and ordinary Christians. Their stories of faith, hope and generosity both challenged and encouraged me. Please come along!

Chapter 2

Why are the Poor, Poor?

Eva

The day I visited Eva she was reeling from the one mile trip she had just made from the nearest river to draw 20 liters of water, barely enough to make one meal for her family. This is a trip that Eva has made for years at least twice a day. A widow and 62 years old, Eva is relatively healthy and has lived in the rural SE part of Kenya since she was a child. She has had ten children and twenty grandchildren. Several years ago, she lost her only gainfully employed son and his wife to AIDS. The three children that they left behind are being sponsored through Tumaini. Nick, one of the orphans, is HIV positive. He is also resilient and a very optimistic boy. He believes that God will help him to beat the AIDS disease.

Apart from the basic support that Eva and three of her grandchildren receive from Tumaini, she relies on subsistence farming on her three acre plot that she is now planning on subdividing among her sons' families. She has a few goats and two oxen that help her till the land. Too often, however, the rains fail to bring meaningful yields so hunger is a perennial reality in her family and the entire village. Despite the fact that her extended family loves and cares for each other, they all suffer the same economic setbacks and no one is able to help each other much.

Talking with Eva, one is easily impressed by her optimistic demeanor and would never guess there was a problem. Like most other poor people in Kenya, she is a happy grandmother who is grateful for the many blessings that God has bestowed her despite the circumstances. Materially speaking, she is very poor but she has an untold reservoir of spirituality that has been inculcated through her church that she faithfully attends.

Fatuma

Back in Nairobi in the slums of Mathare, one of the largest slums in Africa housing between 500,000 to 800,000 people, I met Fatuma. A 36 year old widow and mother of three boys, Fatuma is one of the most optimistic women I met in the slums. She lost her husband four years ago and was left to take care of her three kids alone. When her husband died from AIDS complications which also left her sickly, many of Fatuma's friends in the slums deserted her. She was left alone and sick, basically left to die and leave her kids behind on the unforgiving streets of Mathare. For the first few years, she was forgotten and reduced to a statistic waiting to die and be counted as one of the unfortunate 300 AIDS victims who die daily in Kenya. It was in this state that someone introduced her to a local Christian agency called the Community Transformers, founded by a local orphan who wanted to make a difference in his community. Community Transformers (CT) staff literally came and took Fatuma from her death bed to the hospital. Within a year, Fatuma gained weight after being on ARV's (anti-retroviral medication). CT not only helped her get a good measure of her health back but they also helped her start a small business. It turned out that Fatuma used to sell groundnuts in her neighborhood before she fell sick. So, CT helped her with a small capital loan to re-start. However, she faces another dilemma. Her youngest son who is nine years old can only attend school when Fatuma can afford the $20.00 needed for his fees and tuition. But even then, school is a secondary priority because she needs his help on a daily basis to run her small business, just for basic survival. Only with her son's help can Fatuma be able to put food on the table for her family. Despite this tough situation I was captivated by Fatuma's gratitude to God for bringing CT to her. Life, she says, could have been worse.

Community Transformers had given her hope. The day I visited Fatuma in her ramshackle home in spring 2009, I was accompanied by three staff members of the CT ministry. Sitting on her bed (it doubles as chairs) in her dark, 10' by 10' house I was looking at her feeble body and watching as they commented about the "old bad days that were now behind them." I kept wondering how bad her situation must have been when they first came to her rescue. To see their joy was a sure reminder of God's love and how he had raised these young people and brought them to Fatuma's life. Such connections to a formerly forgotten and dying widow can only be explained through God's providence and sovereignty. Seeing life in Fatuma's eyes and the pure joy of knowing the Lord was incredible.

But even as we sat and rejoiced with Fatuma that morning in her house, I thought of thousands of other "Fatuma's" that lay forgotten in the expansive slums. That morning as we worshipped and thanked God, I knew that literally a few feet away, there were other poor and sick "Fatuma's" just waiting to die. That thought brought tears to my eyes.

The Reality of Poverty

As I reflect on Eva's and Fatuma's resilience and determination to make ends meet, the all too familiar story of what seems like a vicious circle of poverty became obvious. One couldn't help but wonder how many man hours, for example, that Eva 'wastes' in doing her domestic chores every day, just to keep the family surviving. Making endless trips to the seasonal river to draw water and tilling land that has limited returns, makes one question, *how long can this trend continue*? Why is it that in the 21ˢᵗ century there is still a billion people who lack water, basic healthcare, education and food? What has gone awry? Cultural anthropologists tell us that there is a social need that is met when villagers mingle and share the latest news and gossip, which in turn keeps the balance of social equilibrium. But I wonder, is that good enough reason to leave these poor people in their current condition seemingly forever? I think there is a bigger socio-economic issue that cannot be overlooked.

Turning to Fatuma's situation: on the one hand, it is encouraging to see local initiatives where Africans are coming along to help fellow Africans in their distress. However, it seems that the best efforts by CT are helping Fatuma and her three kids survive, but not truly live. Their groundnuts business is only able to help them raise barely enough money for food. Education, which is believed to be the only ticket out of poverty in much of Africa, is a far cry for Fatuma's children. What happens to her three boys when she eventually dies? How will they feed themselves? Will they ever afford education? How will they survive the slums? A more encompassing question is why is Africa, especially sub-Saharan Africa, the most economically devastated region of the world?

Macro-economic context

In September 2000 the United Nations managed to gather in New York key heads of Western countries to mark the beginning of a new millennium as a launching pad for addressing poverty challenges in developing countries. The political leaders agreed on what became known as the Eight Millennium Development Goals (MDGs) aimed at addressing critical poverty related issues. The 8 MDGs to be met by 2015 are:

(1) Eradicate extreme poverty and hunger
(2) Achieve universal primary school enrollment
(3) Promote gender equality and empower women
(4) Reduce child mortality
(5) Improve maternal health
(6) Combat HIV/AIDS, malaria, and other diseases
(7) Ensure environmental sustainability
(8) Develop a global partnership for developments[7].

These are noble goals and I do not doubt the sincerity of the leaders involved in setting out these global approaches. After all, these are the same leaders who control both the economic and political machineries of the world and are best placed to get the funds to the poor. To their credit, the most developed countries, popularly known as the G8, meet regularly and political interests notwithstanding, the agenda of addressing global poverty is often discussed.

However, the reality is that nine years since that all important meeting, one wonders how the implementation of those noble goals has actually helped the poor. I am familiar with the eloquent, annual progress reports that are issued out of ivory towers and fancy boardrooms. My concern, however, is how these goals are being implemented on the ground. I acknowledge that the trillions of dollars that are poured in poor countries are doing some good. That being said, as one who works at the grassroots level with no help from the government, I cannot help but ask, where does the money go? For example, have Eva's and Fatuma's complex poverty situations been improved as a result of the 8 MDGs? Why it is that poverty has *not been eradicated* or at least mitigated in Eva's and Fatuma's case? Why is it that the *global partnership* advocated by the G8 does not seem to have had any tangible, positive impact in poverty-stricken families such as these? How can we explain the depressing estimates that to date, 25,000 people still die every day from hunger-related illnesses?[8] Why does it seem like the poor are inexorably mired in poverty without any chance of getting out despite the optimism that we hear every day from the political elites?

Where does this disconnect occur between the big money and the humble needs of an untold number of grieving, forgotten African grandmothers and their families and how can this gap be bridged? Why isn't the money trickling down to help Eva in a SE village in Kenya or Fatuma who lives in a conspicuously large slum in Nairobi? Let me tell you what I think has happened.

Planners V. Searchers

William Easterly in his book, *The Whiteman's Burden: Why the West's Efforts to Aid the Rest Have Done So Much Ill and So Little Good*,[9] has discussed extensively the limitations of what he calls the *planners* versus the *searchers* approaches. According to Easterly, the *planners* are mainly the big governments or corporations who assume to have all the answers for every poverty situation in the developing world and basically bring pre-packaged responses to otherwise complex, third world contexts. In a sense, *planners* attempt answers to questions that are not necessarily being asked by the people who would be impacted by their decisions the most, the poor. Many times they pour money with all sincerity into poverty situations but years later, the poor continue to suffer the same economic misfortunes.

The *searchers*, on the other hand, come from the bottom up. In many cases they are local innovators, such as Community Transformers, who are intimately aware of the needs and are better placed to address them comprehensively.

Easterly believes that part of the reason why the third world is still as poor as it was sixty years ago even after the West poured 2.3 trillion dollars into it is because the two groups never worked together to address the needs of the poor in a contextual way. Easterly put it aptly, "...*poverty is a complicated tangle of political, social, historical, institutional, and technological factors*".[10]

World Bank figures show that Africa has been the least successful region of the world in reducing poverty with the number of poor people living in Africa doubling between 1981 and 2005 from 200 million to 380 million.[11] A BBC Panorama report posed these timely questions: Why isn't there more success to show for the billions of pounds which have been spent? And why is it that all too often the aid doesn't get through to the very people it is supposed to be helping?

Ideally, planners must find searchers and coordinate to maximize proper use of resources that are poured annually into the developing world. Of course, there are certain things that only planners (governments) can do such as build infrastructure and political and legal frameworks that protect the rights of its citizenry. On the other hand, searchers are better placed to know the local needs and therefore able to address them effectively and in a timely manner.

Poor Governance and Endemic Corruption

One of the biggest obstacles to developing Africa is the endemic corruption by those entrusted with its leadership. Addressing the issue of lack of economic development in Africa,

George Attey, a Ghanainan economist, puts the situation in very colorful terms. He says that "at some point, even perpetual Afro-optimists would be rudely awakened to the law of diminishing returns: That pumping more and more aid into Africa's leaky bowl to induce gangster regimes to implement reforms will yield less and less in results"[12]. The award winning Sierra Leonean reporter, Sorious Samura, investigated Sierra Leone, Uganda and Kenya (among other African countries) and came to the same conclusion that corruption is the number one factor why aid money never trickles down far enough to help the poorest of the poor. [13]

An Oxford University professor and a former World Bank employee focusing on Africa has identified four traps that have kept 1 billion people, the "bottom billion," poor. These traps include: *the conflict trap, the natural resources trap, the trap of being landlocked with bad neighbors, and the trap of bad governance in a small country*.[14] Sadly, 70% of the bottom billion poor live in Africa.[15]

It is fair to point out that the Western countries are not completely innocent in this malaise. The *big plans* that have failed the poor for decades involve leaders of both the developing nations as well as the West. Deals are made with African leaders who are known to be poor in their leadership skills, lacking vision, and corrupt. Large sums of money are spent on expatriates who end up being paid at the rate of their home countries while working in these poor countries. Kick-backs and exorbitant commissions are taken by the local heads of ministries and departments at the expense of the poor. The selection of contractors is not always transparent as issues of nepotism and tribalism take center stage at the expense of professionalism and accountability. The cumulative result of these deficiencies, coupled with selfishness make for a guaranteed failure in taking the poor out of the poverty quagmire that the majority find themselves in. When you add natural and man-made disasters such as famine, civil unrests, devastated agriculture, collapsed infrastructure and political repression to the equation, it is not hard to see why the poor in many developing nations have been plagued into incredible misery. It is not hard to see why Eva and Fatuma find themselves in situations of impossible poverty.

As the *planners* sit in plush boardrooms to decide on major policy issues, the results have been largely dysfunctional policies that cannot be implemented. Not only because some of these policies are foreign and therefore impractical in most third world contexts, but also because most of the would-be implementers have nothing more than self interest to build empires for themselves and their tribal henchmen.

Needless to say, most well-intended big plans are simply not adequately digested for local consumption. This, plus the fact that too many of the leaders of developing nations do not care enough to put the interest of the poor at the center of their agenda, makes for the disastrous situation we find Eva and Fatuma and at least a billion more like them in today.

Micro-context

In a country where 46% of the population lives on under $1.00 a day,[16] intervention is needed to remedy the situation in Kenya. Indeed, Kenya is one of the 48 countries in sub-Saharan Africa which have earned George Ayittey's dubious distinction of "the least-developed region of the Third World."[17] Among the 162 countries that the United Nations Development Program (UNDP) has ranked in terms of human development, using the Human Development Index (HDI), 28 countries at the bottom of the ranking were all located in sub-Saharan Africa. In its Human Development Report (2003), the UNDP warned that, *"Unless things improve it will take sub-Saharan Africa until 2129 to achieve universal primary education, until 2147 to halve extreme poverty and until 2165 to cut child mortality by two thirds. For hunger no date can be set because the regions situation continues to worsen."* [18]

It is important to note that the Kenyan government has embarked on a very ambitious economic plan to lift the majority of Kenyans out of poverty. These plans are detailed in the document titled, *Kenya Vision 2030*.[19] They spell out the short-term, mid-term and long-term economic recovery plans. One encouraging change is a move towards decentralization of essential services. It must be pointed out, however, that this would not be the first time such ambitious plans have been put forth. In my opinion, what is conspicuously missing in the document is how they plan to address the endemic problem of corruption. It is incredible that in a document that is 200 pages long, only half a page is devoted to accountability and corruption and even then, the subject is given a casual treatment. I find this disappointing. Kenya's biggest problem is not economic potential or lack of qualified personnel to implement necessary programs. For me, the biggest obstacle to addressing poverty is the moral corruption that has eaten into the very fabric of the society, beginning with the top leadership down to the village elders. Most people know nothing but a culture of corruption. In fact, most Kenyans go to government and even private sector offices for service expecting to be asked for a bribe. Every day more financial scandals are reported in all the major newspapers. There are even questions as to whether the regime that took the oath of office in January 2008 was actually voted in or votes were simply stolen and therefore we have an illegitimate government in power.

In 2009, Transparency International ranked Kenya as the third most corrupt country in sub-Saharan Africa.[20] In the same article, the author pointed out that corruption was so entrenched that only one in four Kenyans who reported paying a bribe bothered lodging the complaint with the authorities, raising serious doubts about the effectiveness and the legitimacy of the public offices charged with anti-corruption efforts.[21] A few months later, Transparency International did another survey on corruption specifically targeting the three East African countries of Kenya, Uganda and Tanzania and Kenya took the lead in the corruption index.[22]

The report went on to say that " the ranking of key public service agencies like the Police, Judiciary, immigration departments, local authorities, power utility companies, water ministries and hospitals, indicate the public service is infested with corruption" adding that "corruption in these sectors contributes to deepening poverty and increases the cost of doing business in East Africa. Given the fluidity of international trade, the community has to create the right environment to attract and retain foreign and domestic investments." [23]

It was telling that for his first ever visit to Africa south of the Sahara since becoming the President of United States of America, Barack Obama chose to visit the West Africa country of Ghana and not the birth place of his father, Kenya. When asked 'why Ghana' at the July 2009 G8 summit in Italy, Obama did not mince words. Saying that African countries cannot continue blaming colonialism for their current multi-faced problems, Obama chided its leadership and the entrenched culture of corruption, pointing out that international trade was difficult to carry out in the country because companies "can't operate without paying, in some parts of Africa, a 25% fee off the top in bribes".[24] He then singled out Kenya for its corruption and explained his decision to visit Ghana: "The point I was making was that my father travelled to the United States a mere 50 years ago yet now I have family members who live in villages. They themselves are not going hungry, but they live in villages where hunger is real. This is something I understand in very personal terms. And if you talk to people on the ground in Africa, certainly in Kenya, they will say part of the issue is the institutions aren't working for ordinary people. So, governance is a vital concern that has to be addressed."[25]

Is it Worth It?

Going through these statistics is discouraging to those who want to help Africa. Sometimes I ask myself, is it worth it? Is it worth helping Eva and her family? Is CT making any difference by helping Fatuma in a sea of hopelessness? From a Christian perspective I would have to say, it is worth it, even saving one life. Fortunately, the *searchers* have the freedom, if not the cooperation of the developing countries (certainly that is the case in Kenya) to come alongside and help the poor and the forgotten. As Christians we cannot allow circumstances to change the nature of who we are. I was reminded of a Suffi story that I read in Francis Collins book, *The Language of God*, a while back. The story went something like this:

> *Once upon a time there was an old woman who used to meditate on the bank of the Ganges. One morning, finishing her meditation, she saw a scorpion floating helplessly in the strong current. As the scorpion was pulled closer, it got caught in roots that branched out far into the river. The scorpion struggled frantically to free itself but got more and more entangled. She immediately reached out to the drowning scorpion, which, as soon as she touched it, stung her. The old woman withdrew her hand but, having regained her balance, once again tried to save the creature. Every time she tried, however, the scorpion's tail stung her so badly that her hands became bloody and her face distorted with pain. A passerby who saw the old woman struggling with the scorpion shouted, "What's wrong with you, fool! Do you want to kill yourself to save that ugly thing?" Looking into the stranger's eyes, she answered, "Because it is the nature of the scorpion to sting, why should I deny my own nature to save it?* [26]

The moral of the story is that the prevalence of corruption and other social ills shouldn't stop Christians from doing the right thing. Corruption and all manner of social evils should not change the Christian's nature. Part of a Christian's DNA is to help the poor and the down-trodden. The reality is that as Christians, though we are not of this world, we still live in it. As a leader of a Christian agency, I have the responsibility to run the agency in the most transparent manner in a continent that is not exactly transparent. It is a daily struggle but our focus must be on what God has called us to do and be. As the woman in the story so aptly said, we should not change our nature because of our surroundings. We would be wise to heed Muhammad Yunu's word of advice on government's inability to eradicate poverty. He says that *"institutions and policies that created poverty cannot be entrusted with the task of eliminating it."*[27]

Unless this malaise of corruption and tolerance of inept leadership is comprehensively addressed, big plans and more money will never solve the African continent's problems. Sad as this may sound, unless a new way of doing business is ushered into African governments, we will be talking about another Eva and Fatuma a generation away from today engulfed in similar socio-economic conditions.

Searchers: A Better Option

With all the challenges outlined, I believe that it is the *searchers* who understand the needs of the poor. Ideally, *planners* needs to work with *searchers* (with limited government involvement) to address the needs of the poor.

The work of Community Transformers in Mathare slums and Tumaini in the rural areas of SE Kenya have convinced me that Christian agencies can be effective *searchers* in working with the poor. I must point out though that some Christian agencies and churches have, unfortunately, behaved more like *planners*. Therefore working with the community with a *searcher* mentality is not automatic, but an attitude of mind that must be cultivated with time. Furthermore, it is very easy for a well-meaning group to start well, but with time get engulfed with unnecessary bureaucratic processes which not only consume lots of funds, but ultimately accomplish nothing.

A final word on corruption is in order here. I have learned that God will always show us favor when we serve him even in a most corrupt situation. There is absolutely no need to compromise our Christian standards. I have found that the more the community knows that we genuinely are there for them, the more they will even prevent some of the potential pitfalls in our way. I remember walking on the streets of the Mathare slums with some staff of CT and the people on the streets did not only know them by their names, but kept assuring them of their support and assistance should they need any. It was evident from the interactions on the street that CT had established credibility in the eyes of the slum dwellers. I remember them telling me of an incident where they were being denied permits by the local government officials to open another center. Then one elderly grandmother intervened and they were able to get their paper work in order without bribing anyone. Here we were in the poorest part of town and God raised a poor grandmother to assist a Christian agency out of a potentially corrupt deal. This was a reminder to me that God has his people everywhere. We just need to remain true to our nature.

We should always remember, *"Because it is the nature of the scorpion to sting", we ...."Shouldn't deny my [our] own nature to save it."*

Chapter 3

The Family:
When the Foundation
is Shaken

"Mary"

I first met her in the summer of 2004. That morning a few staff of Tumaini and I were visiting to deliver food supplements and other supplies and see how the five kids we were sponsoring were fairing on. As is the case in much of sub-Saharan Africa, Mary had become a parent again after losing a daughter, a son and a daughter-in-law to AIDS. A widow, Mary was a jovial, bubbly 70 year old widow and grandmother of ten. It didn't take me long to sense the graceful demeanor and stability that this woman brought to this family that had been ravaged by AIDS. Mary had the presence of an African matriarchal figure on whose shoulders all power and security of the extended family was anchored. With the death of her husband ten years earlier- who had been the head of the extended family- Mary assumed the responsibility of approving suitors for the girls in the family, food security, resolving land disputes and all other important decisions in her extended family. Apart from the obvious power that Mary possessed, it was clear that she loved her family as demonstrated by the care that she gave to everyone, especially her orphaned grandchildren. In reality, Mary represented the ideal intergenerational link between her many grandchildren and even a few great-grandchildren and her passing generation in the traditional African village.

When I visited the family in the spring of 2009, almost five years later, I was eager to know how Mary was fairing. I later learned from Tom, one of Mary's grandsons, that the beloved and industrious grandmother had died a few months earlier. I asked the young man how they were coping with life after losing the only adult figure in the immediate family. As Tom proceeded to tell me how tough the transition had been, I could see the emotional effect the loss had caused the kids. In the back of my mind, however, I was reflecting on how Mary's death was not just a loss to her nuclear family, but rather how it reflected a microcosm of what organizations working with AIDS orphans had to grapple with in the death of a generation of grandparents, leaving AIDS orphans yet again with no one to take of them. If left unchecked, I reasoned to myself, the orphans can easily be forgotten again. But I also reminded myself that since time immemorial, the peace and tranquility of the African villages had been maintained through a sanctioned social equilibrium that ensured that everyone was taken care of, regardless of their social status. In Tom's case, there was the consolation that the kids were now under the care of an older sibling. I offered my condolences to Tom and assured him of my prayers as he and his siblings learned to cope without Mary's guidance.

"Ruth"

We now make a transition from the village in SE Kenya where Mary's grandchildren live and move some 58 miles NW to Nairobi, the capital city to meet Ruth. Ruth is a 66 year old grandmother. I visited Ruth in her home-cum-business location in the slums of Mathare, Nairobi in April 2009. Ruth lives with a couple of her orphaned grandchildren in a ramshackle home that is no more than 10 by 10 feet in one of the poorest slums in Africa. There are no reliable statistics but by all accounts, between 500,000 and 800,000 Nairobians call the Mathare slums their home.

It didn't take me long to note that I had just met a staunch Christian. Clearly a lady who has seen more than her fair share of life's challenges, Ruth loves the Lord and carries a most optimistic demeanor. When I visited that morning, I was accompanied by four staff members from Community Transformers who have partnered with Ruth to address some of her needs. Immediately after we entered her shack, she insisted on offering us tea and bread before we could even talk to her about her situation. Even though I understand the gracious African hospitality, I could not help but think that Ruth may have offered us all the food she had in her house for her and her 13 year old granddaughter that day. Yet we ate her food joyfully with her knowing that in her heart and mind, she saw our visit as an opportunity to extend hospitality as a means of bringing blessings to her household.

During the conversation that ensued, I came to learn that Ruth was taking care of her six grandchildren that were left behind by her daughter who had died from AIDS several years back. Community Transformers had also helped Ruth place the two youngest kids in an orphanage in Nairobi, and she had been left to take care of the remaining four. In addition, Community Transformers had helped Ruth start a small income-generating business of selling charcoal to her neighbors. In my small chat with Ruth about selling charcoal vis-à-vis its effect on environment, she laughed it off saying that, environmental degradation was the least of her concerns because at her age, she didn't have the energy to engage in a new business venture. She pointed out that living in the city was a challenge as she did not have extended family that would take care of her grandchildren when she died. With a big smile, however, she said, *"Community Transformers is my family. I know they will bury my remains when I die and take care of my grandkids."*

Inevitable Transition

As I sat back and reflected on the experiences of Mary's and Ruth's families, a couple of themes began to emerge in my mind, mostly in the form of questions. How will Tom and his siblings and cousins manage life without their grandmother? More fundamentally, how do children take care of other children? In the case of Ruth, how is it that despite her visibly unbearable circumstances, she seemed genuinely happy and contented with life? How is it possible for one to remain so optimistic in the face of so much loss and no tangible economic hope for the future? How can she afford to show such gratitude in the face of so much hardship? Why is it so easy for the poor to offer total strangers their only meal?

I see even more fundamental questions. How can we, those of us who are coming alongside to help, do so with minimum interruption of their unfathomable happiness? What is the best way to blend in as part of the family or the extended family and not create new social systems that further destabilize their otherwise tranquil lives? In other words, how can we build on what they have as a bridge to what they need? What can we, the non-poor Christians, learn from the destitute poor who have Christ and seem generous almost to a fault? Do the "Ruth's" of the developing world have genuine faith in God's provision or are they simply naïve and displaying irresponsibility and lack of planning for their families?

The Role of Extended Family in Africa

Grandparents play key roles in the nuclear and the extended families in Africa. It was through advanced age that one acquired wisdom, respect and credibility to lead or be consulted. In many cases, especially due to AIDS, they continue to be the anchors of families. Social studies have shown that orphans reared in foster families and especially with extended relatives fare better developmentally than those reared even in the best orphanages. Detailed information can be found on the *Children Rights Information Network* as well as *United Nations*.[28] Indeed, a number of prominent Christian organizations have been promoting extended family care and community care as a better option for orphans. Two of these organizations are *The Better Care Network: faithbasedcarefororphans.org* and *Viva: Together for Children viva.org.*

However, in Africa, we are being faced by a two-pronged challenge with respect to the role of extended families. First, there is the reality of grandparents becoming parents again. Indeed, even though the core Kenyan worldview of interdependence is still intact, the reality of the bread winners between the ages 24 and 49 dying from AIDS is a major challenge, wrecking the social and economic equilibrium right in the center. In the Tumaini ministry over 70% of the children are taken in by grandparents, usually a widowed grandmother. In the absence of the Western, stream-lined social security system, African seniors relied on their children to take care of them in their old age. For their part, the elderly were sought after to give guidance in important matters of life. With the HIV/AIDS pandemic, however, things have changed and the long held pillars of the traditional society are falling apart. We are in the midst of a tumultuous and ever changing socio-economic and socio-cultural context.

The second challenge is that, in many cases, these grandparents are dying when the orphans are still young and needing parental guidance. The average age of these grandmothers is 72 years. Mary is a case in point. This situation calls for a fresh search for new, viable ways to provide for these forgotten children. It is important that even as we look for ways to take care of these orphans, we do so without taking them away from their families and thus safeguard the integrity of social norms.

In the remainder of this chapter, I will take a closer look at these twin issues- the death of parents first followed by the loss of grandparents- and address them in the context of the role of extended family. Drawing from the case studies of Ruth's and Mary's family, I will show how partnership between Christian agencies and the families affected by the AIDS pandemic can come to the rescue of countless forgotten orphans.

Corporate Connectedness

It is important to provide broad world view parameters that will help the reader appreciate the macro picture of the African setting before we focus on the micro cases of Ruth's and Mary's families. Before we delve deeper into the practical matter at hand, I will provide a theoretical framework of world view, a framework that will help us define the role of the extended families in an African setting.

My work with AIDS orphans has reinforced my belief that the basic framework of social corporate connectedness in Africa is still intact. I use the phrase *corporate connectedness* sociologically to convey the idea or feeling of affinity that a certain people group or groups of people have toward one another. Essentially, it is the idea that they intrinsically 'belong to each other' or 'are all in this together' in good or bad times. For example, in a traditional African village, children 'belong' to the community. All members of the community are therefore socially obligated to take care of 'their' children. It is true that due to post modernity and unabated urbanization, some of the strict traditional world views observed in the villages are being challenged and, in indeed, in serious danger of being replaced with new social networks in major urban centers[29]. Yet at the core of most societies, the idea that we are each other's keeper is not completely lost.

In a previous publication, I identify three levels of corporate connectedness across Africa[30].

First is the *blood* connectedness which comprises members of the nuclear family as well as the extended members. The second level of connectedness is a *social* or *respect* bond. In much of Africa, children address adults as 'aunts' and 'uncles' even where there is virtually no known blood relationship. Here in America, children of many of my friends from across Africa address me as 'uncle.' The third category is *subculture* bonds. Subculture networks are of course universal, but in Africa have been introduced primarily through urbanization and growing post modernity.

The idea of corporate connectedness is entrenched throughout Africa and is given various tribal or regional expressions[31]. In Kenya, for example, the Kiswahili phrase that captures the essence of corporate connected is *wa kwetu*.[32] In essence, *wa kwetu* means "one who is from my home," or "one from my family." John Mbiti of Kenya put it best when he coined the dictum: "I am because we are, and since we are, therefore I am".[33] Writing from a West African context, Austin Echema echoed Mbiti's sentiments: "A person does not stand alone; one's first sense of personal identity is with the community." [34] Today, the concept of *wa kwetu* exists even among the African elites wherever they may be found. It can be observed daily by those of us from the same country or continent when we meet overseas, whether that may be Paris, Frankfurt, London, Los Angeles, Tokyo or Mumbai. In broader sociological terms, *wa kwetu* also applies to subcultures such as club memberships, including church affiliations. For example, people belonging to the same country club, even though they may have no blood relationship would be *wa kwetus*. Similarly, people worshipping in the same church, though from different ethnic groups or races, would be *wa kwetus*. If we push this concept to its natural conclusion, we can say that Christians, all over the world belong to the same family, the same *wa kwetu*, the family of God.

Corporate Connectedness in Contemporary Society

As I have grappled with the reality of dying grandparents, I have increasingly found that our answer to continued care of the orphans may lie in the elastic concept of *wa kwetu*. Indeed, with the death of grandparents, I have witnessed corporate connectedness at play. While it is true that the death of a loving grandmother, such as Mary leaving behind Tom and his siblings and cousins without an adult in the nuclear family is incredibly painful, it is amazing how many 'uncles', 'aunts' and other relatives are often able to step in and fill the vacuum. It is these social networks wherein lies hope for these otherwise forgotten children. Within the confines of the African *wa kwetu* is hospitality and care for one another, especially the weak and vulnerable. Despite the greed and selfishness witnessed among the powerful in society, the majority of Africans do truly care for the weak and feeble. Indeed, without these networks, most of the 11 million AIDS orphans in Africa would be in far worse situations. I have witnessed total strangers very poor by all standards drawing from the deep wells of their generosity and giving whatever they can afford to assist their needy neighbors. Such poor yet caring people just need a hand-up to help raise their families, not hand-outs.

Western Donors and Corporate Connectedness

Since 2004, I have led nearly thirty Vision Trip teams from the U.S. to Kenya. Many times, these types of trips attract donors interested in meeting their sponsored children. I have witnessed countless situations where kids after meeting with their donors for the first time immediately address them as 'Mum' or 'Dad.' That is why a visit by a donor to their sponsored children leaves an indelible mark in the life of the kids. I have two girls that I sponsor--a 21 year old and a 17 year old. They both call me 'dad' and my wife 'mom'. They call our three sons 'brothers' and they call each other 'sister' although there is no biological relationship in either case. Another 17 year old girl that my wife sponsors calls us 'mom' and 'dad' respectively and calls our sons her 'brothers.' She and the other two girls call each other 'sisters'.

Many times, my American friends are caught off guard because they do not necessarily see these children as their kids. Yes, they love them, give money for their support and pray for them regularly, but they do not necessarily think of them as their own children. This is understandable given the world view differences between Africa and Western societies [35]. Sometimes, I have seen my American friends become a little uneasy, embarrassed or simply unsure of how to respond when the children refer to them as 'mom and dad'. I completely understand because I know that things in the West are stated in white and black. Not so in Africa. Reality is explained in blurred terms and relationships are interwoven in what world renowned anthropologist the late Paul Hiebert used to call "fuzzy sets." [36] By "fuzzy sets", Hiebert was referring to relationships that are not defined in typical Western categories. In the West, the term *cousin* or *brother* has a definite blood relationship connotation. Not so in Africa. In the African context, a *cousin* or *brother* may be someone who has a clan or totem relationship but no blood relationship whatsoever. However, such a person is no less a *cousin* or *brother* in that setting.

As the years have gone by, I have noticed that, by and large, the idea that sponsors are actually parents to these forgotten orphans is beginning to sink in. As they have begun to understand the concept from the child's perspective, I have witnessed donors welling up with tears when they receive letters from 'their kids' in Africa. Larretta, one of the 'moms' from

Yuma, Arizona summed up her experience this way: *"Our small groups wait for letters from their children while faithfully praying for them each time they meet. And it is those letters that tug at our heartstrings. To be called Mum and Dad by children most have never met... in Kenya is indeed life changing."*[37] With time donors have begun to realize that they may be the only loving parents that the children know. In their world view, the orphans are no longer orphans. The orphans know that that they are no longer forgotten because they now have parents, brothers, sisters, aunts and uncles, only that they live some 8000 miles away.

I do not want to oversimplify an otherwise complex issue but it is amazing how despite the world view differences, God keeps bridging the gap between the Western donor and the African orphan. What this is teaching me is that at the end of the day, despite our temporal differences, we are all God's children and each called to play a different role in the drama that God is orchestrating in his heavenly dwellings.

One of the things I observed when we visited Ruth is that even though she had lost her daughter and had no extended family in the city, she was confident that even after she died, her grandchildren will be taken care of by her Christian family, her brothers and sisters of Community Transformers. Though aware that most of these kids would never have gone to school had it not been for outside intervention, she kept going back to why she was happy. She said *"I know the world cannot watch my entire family perish in hunger, they have always shared the little they have with me."* One could reason that this was just a naïve statement because we have read of people dying of hunger in Kenya within the past few years. But Ruth's statement must be understood in the context of interdependence. She felt home in this urban *wa kwetu*, the Christian sub-culture. She truly sees Community Transformers as her extended family. Though some of the donors to CT live 8,000 miles away, as far as Ruth is concerned, she has this elastic view of family. What a faith!

The People of God as Extended Family

A common metaphor in the Bible is the description of the people of God or the church as family. This can be seen from both in the Old and New Testaments of the scriptures. For example, the family unit is a basic part of the structure of creation. Right from the beginning, we see God's purpose for humanity was to live as family (Adam, Eve and their children). Later in the Genesis account, the significance of the family is even more pronounced for it lies at the center of God's purpose. We read in Genesis 12:2-3 the following: *"I will make you a great nation; I will bless you and make your name great; and you shall be a blessing. I will bless those who bless you, and I will curse him who curses you; and in you all the families of the earth shall be blessed." (NKJV)* As the biblical story of Abraham continues to unfold, we begin to see the fulfillment of this grand promise. Abraham's family grows from his son Isaac to his grandson Jacob, whose name ("Israel") becomes the very name by which the people of God are known. Indeed, the history of what became the 'people of God' can best be viewed as an expansion of the family of Abraham and his wife Sarah. It is through this family that the whole world is to be blessed or cursed.

Under the Abrahamic covenant, *"the family is thus a theological as well as a biological and social structure…it is through membership in a covenant family that the child is related to the covenant people of God"*[38] Thus, symbolically, Abraham becomes the founder of a new covenant people. The implications of this truth are far reaching when we think of Mary's grandchildren in the village of SE Kenya and Ruth's family in the heart of Mathare slums in Nairobi. By virtue of their faith in God, they and their donors in the US belong to the same family, God's family. The people of God, wherever they may be found belong to the same family. We are *wa kwetu. Wa kwetu* calls us to remember that we are our brothers' and sisters' keeper wherever the brother and sister may be found on the globe.

Jesus' View on Family

Jesus who is genealogically a descendant of Abraham fulfills the old promise that 'all nations of the earth will be blessed through him.' Through his life's ministry and death on the cross, Jesus unites all believers, Jews and Gentiles, to their common father and head of the family—God the Father. Central to Jesus' ministry is the call to his followers to love one another, to live as new people with a common father. He goes on to suggest a radical way of viewing what a family is. For example, in Mark 10:29-30 Jesus describes the family of God as leaving our original families and forming new ones. It says, *"Truly, I say to you, there is no one who has left house or brothers or sisters or mother or father or children or lands, for my sake and for the gospel, who will not receive a hundred fold now in this time- house, and brothers and sisters and mothers and children and lands, with persecutions- and in the age to come eternal life."* It is significant to note that the concept of family is not lost. Rather, what we have is *a new family*. This is crucially important in terms of our central focus, corporate connectedness. Jesus is advocating for a new *wa kwetu*, a new family whose membership is followership of Christ irrespective of race, language, culture, skin color or any other social differentiations. Jesus is calling his disciples to transcend their human family, *wa kwetu* relationships and think of all believers wherever they may be found as family.

Paul's View on Family

The same theme of one family is carried on by the apostle Paul, especially in his epistle to the Ephesians. In chapter 2, the Jewish and Gentile Christians who were previously alienated from one another, are now to live together. Making a reference to Christ, Paul reminds the Ephesian Christians that, *"through him we both have access in One Spirit to the Father. So then you are no longer strangers and sojourners, but you are fellow citizens with the saints and members of the household of God"* (2:18-19). Through the death of Christ, there was both a vertical and horizontal reconciliation which can be easily understood in a *wa kwetu* setting. In Romans 8:16-17 Paul states explicitly that Christians are *"children of God, and if children, then heirs, heirs of God and fellow heirs with Christ."* Elsewhere, Paul speaks movingly of his relationship with other 'family members.' For example, he gives instruction on how Christians are to treat weaker neighbors, describing the relationship as that of a *"brother for whom Christ died."* (I Cor. 8:11, 13) Writing to Philemon about Onesmus, he talks of him as his 'child' whose 'father' he 'became.' Other epistles are replete with such family references and this gives us the idea of the apostle's mindset on the inclusive nature of Christian faith.

A Glimpse of Hope

Ruth was right when she told me that she was confident that when she dies, her extended family- the people of God- will be there for her grandchildren. That statement in itself was good enough. But something else special happened that morning. I watched carefully the interaction between Ruth and the Community Transformers staff. You see, Ruth comes from a tribe that was at the center of political controversy following the infamous elections in Kenya in Dec. 2007[39] and the vicious tribal war that followed. Most of the staff members of Community Transformers, on the other hand, come from the tribe that fought with Ruth's tribe. Both tribes had lost so many members of their respective communities and therefore remained bitter with open animosity between the two tribes. Yet, in this house this particular morning, these believers genuinely embraced each other in love. Nobody talked about politics or revenge that morning. They all pointed to the one common enemy that they are trying to defeat. They talked about the AIDS pandemic and how to best address its aftermath as believers of one family, the family of God. For me, these believers demonstrated what it means to belong to one family, the family of God, a *new wa kwetu*. I thought to myself, perhaps the Church had not been completely tainted by the politics of the day as much as I had thought. Maybe if Christians in Africa embraced this *sub-culture wa kwetu* and de-emphasized the importance of the *blood wa kwetu* there can be healing in the continent. Maybe if Christians embraced this kind of *wa kwetu* and saw themselves as the family of God, regardless of which country we come from or which ethnic group we belonged to, perhaps we can take better care of the 11 million AIDS orphans in Africa. That morning, I truly saw a glimpse of hope for the forgotten orphans.

Grief:
When it is OK to Cry

"Joey"

Over the years I have had many interactions with Joey. He wears a great smile and his sense of purpose and responsibility is unmatched by most 21 year olds that I know. On March 2, 2008, Joey and I had a long conversation about his life and how God had blessed him so much in spite of his parents' deaths. For some reason we found ourselves talking about how he felt when his parents died. Prior to this date Joey and I had never really talked about the details of how he felt about his parents death; we had a couple of hours and we got to talking.

He began to tell me the agony he felt when his dad died in 2000. He told me that when his father passed, he pretty much concealed his emotions and didn't take time to grieve because, as he put it, "I had to be strong for my (then) ailing mom, a young sister and grand mom". A year later, when his mother died, he also didn't grieve because as he said, "I had to be strong for my sister and grandmother." At this point, Joey fell silent for a couple of minutes and then he began to cry uncontrollably. As he continued to sob, I became concerned because I didn't know what the people sitting across from us were thinking about us or what had happened to Joey.

Like in some other cultures, men in most African communities aren't supposed to cry, at least not in public. Though only 16 years old at the time of his dad's death, Joey became the man of the house and he saw it as his responsibility to take care of his ailing mother, his sister and their grandmother.

It took Joey seven years to shed tears and to consciously begin to process his parents' death. I am not a psychologist or psychiatrist so I cannot pretend to know the challenges that someone goes through when they lose their parents at such an early age. All I know is that, for some reason, Joey felt comfortable enough this particular day to let out the emotions and finally begin the grieving process.

"Grace"

In the spring of 2009, I sat down with Grace and asked her to share how she was fairing on since her mom's death. I have known Grace since the time she was in junior high school and her cautious demeanor tells the story of a troubled past. Even before we started the conversation I knew that I was in the presence of a delicate and raw soul that was in the process of a long road to recovery.

During a two hour long conversation, Grace began by saying, "…I have been given a sense of care, love and concern that I had never known before. Because of my poor health, I think I have received more attention than most of the other kids. Tumaini spend (sic) so many funds on me and I really can't say enough about how grateful I am."

Grace continued: "Hope is what Tumaini has brought into my life. Before Tumaini came in, I was so cornered by life. But almost instantly, I was rejuvenated and I got my life back as it was slowly sliding away from me. I was given a chance to continue in school and in life in general."

She then proceeded, between sobs, to narrate her horrific childhood experience: *"When my mom died, I was 8 years old and among my siblings (a brother and two sisters), I was affected the most. I used to cry every day and really didn't understand what was going on. It has been 13 years since mom's death but I still miss her very much. Having some extended family members who have been very abusive (including physical abuse) complicated things even more. One of them called me the most derogative thing you could call a child in Kenya, "chokora".[40] Although this happened more than six years ago, I still shiver with fear when I remember such characterization by an adult. I think the biggest damage is that this kind of insult has caused me to fear all men in general and I am afraid that it may affect my future relations with men. Tumaini has been very helpful in assisting me address this very damaging psychological reality that I have had to deal with. The fact that I am sharing this incident is a testament to the work of grace that God is doing in my life through counseling on this aspect of my life."*

Grace concluded with these hopeful words: "Tumaini has changed me. Tumaini has taught me that there are still people out there who care and love the forgotten, suffering orphans. I feel loved and cared for and I have been given hope beyond my wildest dreams."

I left the interviewing room with a sobering feeling. I felt as hurt as Grace did except that hers was a reality that she had lived through, mine was just sympathy. How can one empathize with a story that sad? Why would innocent orphans suffer so much? I found myself saying very little during the entire session. Really, no words I could think of would reverse Grace's situation.

"Julie"

An outstanding leader in her own right, Julie shared how far she had come in her healing process. Julie narrated the agonizing experience of watching her parents die within a couple of years. "Dad passed away in 2001 and mom in 2002 when I was 12 years old. My parents had separated so Dad's death didn't hit me as hard. Initially, my parents death, especially my mom's, didn't seem real. In reality, I didn't accept my mom's death until 2006 when I was a junior in high school. All of a sudden it hit me that I was alone and I became very moody. This psychological state affected my relationships as well as my academic performance. It hurt the most at school when other students talked about their parents. It really hurt me when the reality hit that I will never have that experience [of being loved by parents] again. I slowly began to realize that I had never accepted my mom's death."

Julie's healing process began with her Tumaini sponsorship: "… Tumaini is like a second home to me. It gives me the feeling that I am at home. My leadership gifts have blossomed at Tumaini. First, I was appointed the deputy head girl, then the head girl and now as a counselor. It has been an honor being part of Tumaini. It has been a privilege. I see Tumaini as my home. Tumaini gives me a sense of belonging. I don't have to mind how I look, dress or anything else because I am at home where I am loved. In fact, when I compare Tumaini with my other homes— grandparents, aunts, uncles, brother, sister, etc, I feel most comfortable at Tumaini."

Julie shared how coming to Tumaini had been therapeutic, "not only because I received counseling but especially that I met others who had similar experiences of having lost parents like me." Sobbing, she shared a very moving experience she had at a Tumaini Christian camp: "I met and fell in love with a small boy by the name Kakai. This boy had lost his mom when he was a baby and to see his grace gave me reason to come back to Tumaini and help counsel him so that he doesn't have to delay his mourning as I had done. Tumaini has really become a family where we help each other deal with our deep emotional wounds. During the TUBE [Tumaini Bible Experience] week, our traumatic experiences are addressed. In my junior year in high school, I felt like a sponge whose water had been squeezed out completely. TUBE and other sessions changed that completely."

"Lois"

Lois is 22 year old university student majoring in Math and Business. One should not mistake her diminutive stature for a timid girl. With piercing eyes and a sharp, inquisitive mind, Lois has her heart set on great things. A few years ago, such lofty goals would have been but distant dreams. Like others, Lois came to Tumaini having lost her loving parents and very much wounded, forgotten and traumatized. Of her healing process, she told me the following: "At the TUBE I found out that I was not alone in orphan hood. I met many other kids who had also lost parents and through sharing and focused counseling, I developed a healthy attitude to life." What helped with Lois's healing process the most was the self-discovery that bad as her loss was, there were kids who had suffered even more. She confessed: "I actually found there were some kids who were in worse situations than I was. Some had no clothes, no relatives or anyone in their family who cared. The worst were cases where kids were too young to remember how their parents looked like before they died." Understandably, Lois gets emotional when she talks about the kids who cannot remember their parents. It is actually these kids who have challenged her the most and led to her becoming a Tumaini camp counselor herself. "This really touched me and that is why I love serving as a counselor to help other kids recover from their traumatic experiences and begin to live their lives to the fullest just as I have."

"Liz"

With a broad and contagious smile, the 23 year old Liz comes across as a shy girl. In talking with her one quickly realizes the cause for shyness. "You see my parents had died from AIDS and people were afraid of us", she told me, adding, "My sisters and I were treated as if we had no worth and we felt the same. This experience made me to completely lose my confidence for a long time." The more I talked with Liz, the more I became convinced that there was something deeper in this young woman than the raw emotions she was letting out. I realized that she is a woman of deep reflection and determination. Despite her apparently shy nature, she is one of the few people in Africa that I have met who is not ashamed or afraid to talk openly about AIDS and how the disease killed her parents. Such an open admission is the beginning of the long recovery.

A recent university graduate preparing to enter Christian ministry, Liz is determined to give back to the community. Commenting on her healing process, she quipped: "My self-esteem has increased. Prior to being part of Tumaini, I thought I was the only orphan. But by getting to know other orphans has caused my confidence to increase. I had given up hope… As part of Tumaini family, I have not only received counseling but have been able to counsel others to come out the embarrassing mode and live out their lives to the fullest in Christ."

As one who is recovering, Liz is able to empathize with others' situations. Like Julie and Lois, sharing her experiences with younger orphans who have a longer way to go in their healing process has been a mutual blessing. Their experiences remind me of an African saying, ukuu ukulawa uwakwiiwe, which translates something like this: "the best counseling to the bereaved can only come from those who have been bereaved." In other words, it is those who have been emotionally wounded and have found healing who can best bring healing to others.

As I consider the unfortunate emotional journeys that these five young adults have gone through, four themes begin to emerge. They seem to be at a cross-roads; they have become wounded healers; they teach us that emotional healing is a long process; and they affirm the reality and place for a new family (wa kwetu) –the church or the people of God as beacon of hope for the otherwise forgotten orphans.

Life Cross-roads

As already observed in a previous chapter, some of the cultural pillars in the African traditional societies are facing unprecedented challenges. In some irreversible ways, the society is transitioning from operating solely on the traditional wa kwetu blood bonds and moving more intentionally toward social and sub-cultural bonds. One of the unintended consequences of this transition is that unless other measures are taken, AIDS orphans who are by default left under the care of grandmothers are eventually left alone and forgotten when the grandparents die. The result is a forgotten generation who, without intervention can lose all. As the African adage says, "When two elephants fight, it is the grass that gets trampled." In this case, one elephant is HIV/AIDS and the other elephant is the death of the grandparents. When the dust settles, the orphans are left alone. Who is to come and stand by these lovely children as they process the deaths of their loved ones and navigate life to become adults themselves? So far, the few stories narrated here point to the critical role the people of God have played in bringing about the healing. What an opportunity for the people of God to do the very thing that God calls his church to do: serve the orphans and widows as the only true religion that God accepts!

Cultural Disconnect

Although I never lost my parents in such a traumatic fashion, as a cultural insider, I can relate to the experiences of these young men and women when it comes to most African forms of mourning and how they affect the young members of society. I vividly remember when my grandfather died, even though he had lived a full life (died at an estimated age of 120), the morning after he died all of us kids were asked to go to the field and tend to animals. Nobody told us that grandpa had died. I remember seeing elderly and respected men from the surrounding villages milling about in our compound and gathering in small groups. I knew something was amiss because they were talking in hushed voices. They did not want the rest of the family to know except men. This was not unusual. Many times the rest of the family learned of a death only after the body had been disposed of. Traditionally, men were seen as the protectors of women and children from all harm and unnecessary emotional trouble. Even after burying a loved one, sometimes the children were simply told that so and so had left for another village. Of course, the children eventually found out and their mourning would begin then.

So when Joey, Grace, Julie, Lois and Liz told me that they were the last ones to actually find out about their parents' deaths, I knew exactly the cultural dynamics at play at the time. In Joey's case, he was let to know earlier compared to Grace and Julie by virtue of being a boy and the new head of the family, so to speak. But even in his case, they didn't tell him about his mom's death until all the adult relatives had been informed and plans were underway to bury her. Grace knew nothing about mom's death until days after. In reality, Grace hasn't really processed her mom's death yet. Julie was not informed directly about mom's death and that is probably why it took her years to accept her death.

Imperfect as that cultural system is, there is at least a clearly defined way of dealing with grief. The only problem is that times have changed. In traditional African societies, everyone lived in the village and there were social avenues to deal with grief in a collective version. Within the last thirty years or so, the cultural pillars of society that had developed and perfected the system have been dying off. Modernity, urbanization and now post modernity have set in and slowly replaced the role of informal education which was passed from generation to generation. Of course, there is no other disease in the recent past that has claimed the lives of the most productive age sector (15-49) than AIDS has. So we are in a new day with new dilemmas.

What is more is that fact that Africa has wholeheartedly (and uncritically) embraced all that the western world has to offer, including dealing with loss and grief. The one problem with such an approach is that while much of Africa has embraced these western methods of doing things, including grief counseling, I don't believe we have fully understood the western approaches and digested them for local consumption. Here is one glaring example. In the western setting, it is very normal to hug or somehow show publicly sympathy when someone is bereaved. Indeed, western counselors encourage it and actually say that is part of the healing process. In many African societies, people don't hug liberally and even in contexts where it is done, it depends on who is allowed to hug whom. I remember bringing a team of my America friends to meet my mom in Kenya in 2005 after I had lost a brother. We visited for about two hours and as we were about to leave, someone on the team said to me, "Stanley, why didn't you hug your mom? It's been months since you last saw her and she lost a son, your brother not too long ago!" I had to explain that I loved my mother and wanted to hug her but that would have been the first time that I ever hugged her. My friend countered: "But I hugged her and she seemed happy with it." Smiling I said, "Yes I saw that!" The truth is, part of me wanted to hug my mom, but another part of me was conscious that this would be very awkward. My American friend accepted my answer but I could see that she was baffled by the whole experience. I doubt that I am alone in this dilemma.

On the other hand, we in Africa are quickly abandoning our old ways (such as the traditional mourning process). The result is that we are neither fully Africans anymore and of course, not westerners but a half-baked continent. That is actually how I felt the morning my American friend confronted me about not hugging my mom. This is not only true in terms of grieving processes. It is also true in politics, government, education, religion and so forth. I believe that since we cannot go back to where we were before the western influence, the best way forward is to critically contextualize the services we offer so that they meet the needs of the 21st century Africans, may that be in politics or church. I believe that sub-culture wa kwetu is the way to go and this includes addressing loss and grief among the AIDS orphans.

Just a word about the five individuals I have covered in this chapter. Liz has already graduated from college and moved on. Joey, Julie and Lois are university students and no longer live in the homogenous setting in the village. Grace is waiting to join college in the near future. In reality, they cannot rely on the traditional family wa kwetu for their needed healing. Their only hope is a sub-culture wa kwetu. This is where I see the church of Jesus Christ presented with an amazing opportunity to become family to millions of these AIDS orphans.

Wounded Healers

Despite their unspeakable level of loss and emotional struggles in a culturally fluid time, the likes of Joey, Grace, Julie, Lois and Liz are an incredibly resilient lot. They have demonstrated time and again that given a hand-up, they can pick up the pieces and actually become incredibly responsible men and women. Indeed, they are not only able to pick up the pieces and make something of their otherwise damaged lives but are also able and willing to reach out to others who are even more forgotten than themselves.

In his insightful 2007 book, *Wounded Healer*, Henri Nouwen makes the point that "ministers' sufferings makes for good material in bringing the counselees closer to God." As I have reflected on the stories of Joey, Grace, Julie and Lois, particularly how far they have come in their emotional and social growth, I cannot help but see in them wounded healers. Yes, even after many years since their parents' death, in many aspects their wounds are still very raw. Yet, the confidence that they exude and their deep faith in God makes them excellent healers. As we saw earlier, these young adults now serve out of experience, out of the victories they have experienced so far in their lives. Julie had this to say about a counseling the young Kakai, "This boy had lost his mom when he was a baby and to see his grace gave me reason to come back to Tumaini and help counsel him so that he doesn't have to delay his mourning as I had done." Lois was moved to serve as a counselor when she found out that there were some orphans who had suffered more than she. Said Lois, "This really touched me and that is why I love serving as a counselor to help other kids recover from their traumatic experiences and begin to live their lives to the fullest just as I have."

I think there is something to be said about transformed lives and their impact on those who suffer. The positive lives of Joey, Julie and Lois reminds me of Paul's words to the church at Corinth where he writes, "He comforts us in all our troubles so that we can comfort others. When they are troubled, we will be able to give them the same comfort God has given us. For the more we suffer for Christ, the more God will shower us with his comfort through Christ. Even when we are weighed down with troubles, it is for your comfort and salvation! For when we ourselves are comforted, we will certainly comfort you. Then you can patiently endure the same things we suffer. We are confident that as you share in our sufferings, you will also share in the comfort God gives us." 2 Cor 1:4-7 (NLT)

Although Tumaini has many Christian counselors who work with the orphans as they deal with their emotional wounds, it has become apparent that the most effective counselors are those who have themselves suffered the loss of parents but have considerably processed their grief. In some ways, they have come to terms with life as it is and are best equipped to counsel others undergoing the same emotional roller coaster.

Talking about the joy of counseling younger orphans, Julie shares an interesting breakthrough she had with other orphans at a Tumaini Christian camp recently: "During TUBE week, I have noticed that kids don't like talking about the death of their parents both because AIDS is a stigma and also because it reminds the kids of a subject they want to forget. It is like nailing metal in a raw wound! In Dec. 2008, I had a privilege to serve as counselor for grades 7 & 8. It was amazing how God used my experience of 'accepting' my mom's passing in speaking to their needs as well. I found out that just by sharing one's experiences, it opened their hearts and made them willing to deal with their own situations as well." Julie went on to share how one kid had asked a question about remembering parents and God used her own experience in addressing the question.

Julie's testimony has been shared by countless other Tumaini kids who although they are still processing their emotional challenges, they have become the most effective in reaching others in similar situations. Isn't this the same thing we as Christians have experienced with Jesus! When we experience temptations, grief or suffering of any nature he is able to emphathize with us because he has been there before. Consider, for example, these words by the writer of Hebrews 4: "This High Priest of ours understands our weaknesses, for he faced all of the same testings we do, yet he did not sin. So let us come boldly to the throne of our gracious God. There we will receive his mercy, and we will find grace to help us when we need it most." (NLT)

The Long Journey to Healing

The five experiences discussed in this chapter are a microcosm of similar life stories that are a reality to millions of AIDS orphans all over Africa and possibly beyond.

For most of them, the road has been long and rough yet it is amazing how such stories have turned out for the better as the kids get involved in the lives of others in similar circumstances in Christian environments. It is amazing how such varied and turbulent beginnings find a common course and how Christian intervention has brought hope to the victors and those around them. It is refreshing how such forgotten kids have found hope and peace and how quick they want to extend it to others.

I found it interesting to dig deeper into the psychological process that grieving children go through after the loss of parents. Harvard child psychology professor J. William Worden has identified four tasks of the mourning process that all bereaved individuals go through.

Task 1: …there is always the delicate balance between wishing that it had not happened, or that the deceased will return, and the reality of the loss." [41]

Task 2: …feelings of ambivalence and responsibility. If a highly ambivalent relationship existed between the child and the deceased parent prior to the death, one often finds considerable anger, frequently expressed in feelings of abandonment such as 'why did he [or she] leave me?' Ambivalent relationships may also lead children to feel responsible for the death because of something they did or did not do or say."[42]

Task 3: ...the mother is frequently the emotional caretaker of the family as well as the child's confidante. An aspect of the mourning process includes adapting to the loss of these roles, which have died with the mother." (pg 15)

Task 4: "The child must be helped to transform the connection to the dead parent and to a place the relationship in a new perspective, rather than to separate from the deceased."[43]

Although William Worden did his research in a western context, it is amazing how similar children experiences are once they loose their parents. This study gives us a hint as to the complex mourning process that AIDS orphans go through. In retrospect, I can see why after many years since she was called a 'chokora' Grace cries uncontrollably to this day. I can see why even after 13 years, because of her attachment to her mother, Grace has not fully accepted her death. Although I can't understand it, I can see why Julie was in denial of her mother's death for years. In many ways, I see her mourning her mom to this day. I can see why Joey even after concealing his emotions for many years, had to let go and release some emotions. Professor Worden's next comment makes a lot of sense. "The child bereavement study has extended our knowledge of the way in which children maintain an ongoing connection to the death parent. Through a process we call 'constructing' the deceased, the child develops an inner representation of the dead parent that allows him or her to maintain a relationship with the deceased, a relationship that changes as the child matures and in the intensity of grief lessens. The child negotiates and renegotiates the meaning of the loss, and in time, relates the dead person in his or her life and memorializes that person in a way that allows life to move on."[44]

Coming to terms with death is never easy. The difference is that in the western context, there are well defined counseling processes that are time tested to help when grief hits. In Africa, however, we are at a cross-roads, having abandoned the traditional systems of grief and not yet fully digesting the western methods that we are trying to embrace. It is a real opportunity for the church in Africa to step in and provide a much needed and suitable functional substitute.

In her book, *Parenting Through Crisis*,[45] Barbara Coloroso provides a helpful insight regarding the process of grief. She says for example that "there is no destination, no arrival, and no ending place in the journey of grief. There is no roadmap to follow, no formula, and no way to hurry the journey or bypass the pain. There are passages to pass through, not stages that we move past in a lockstep, hierarchical order. To force ourselves or our children into a linear grieving 'process,' evaluating where we are on the ladder of grief, is a vain attempt to control and manipulate a 'journey of the heart.' This journey cannot be controlled; it can only be lived through by each one of us in our own time and in our own ways." [46]

I found Coloroso's admission both frustrating but at the same time helpful. It is frustrating because in life, we want a game plan that has an endpoint. We don't want to do the same thing all the time with no results in hand. When something bad happens to us, we want to address it and get back total control of our lives within the shortest time possible. Yet I found it helpful because it acknowledges the reality of human psyche. We are a complex species and there are no microwave-fast quick fixes to our emotional wounds.

This realistic assessment helps us begin to understand Grace and Julie when they admit that even after several years they are still processing the fact that their moms are dead. Overcoming grief is a process and we cannot rush to the endpoint. Perhaps as Christians we can learn how to process this reality better by looking at the Apostle Paul's situation. At one point he admitted to the Christians at Corinth that he had accepted a certain 'thorn in his flesh' as the new normal for him. This is how he put it: "…So to keep me from becoming proud, I was given a thorn in my flesh, a messenger from Satan to torment me and keep me from becoming proud. Three times I begged the Lord to take it away, each time he said, 'My grace is all you need. My power works best in weakness. So now I am glad to boast in my weaknesses so that the power of Christ can work through me." (2 Corinthians 12, NLT)

Since emotional healing is such a long journey, a journey of a lifetime for some, it is a stark reminder for us to rely more on God. God says that human beings are wonderfully made and so who better to understand even our deepest psyches than the Creator himself.

Forging a New family

I once asked a psychologist friend of mine the time line for AIDS orphans to get healed emotionally. He emphatically suggested that there may not be such a thing as complete healing. He said that the best that we can hope for is a healthy appreciation of their new reality to a point where they can live normally and be productive members of society.

Here is where the church of Jesus Christ comes in. Yes, as Africa transitions from traditional to modern and post-modern modes of dealing with grieving, this is where God's love must be demonstrated. It is instructive that in all the five cases cited above, the breakthrough to their healing journey was not found in a counselor's office. They each only opened up to Christian brothers and sisters who showed them love and concern over their lives. As they each said, for the first time in their lives (since the parents passed), they met Christians who really cared.

I do admit that there is a place for professional counseling because there are deeply seated issues that the untrained are not adequately equipped to handle. But grieving cannot be fully dealt with outside of the Christian environment. Christians, no matter their cultural or professional backgrounds have something special that these young adults need. Take the example of Michelle. A native of Southern California, Michelle has been to Kenya eight times so far! Each time she leads a vision trip. Her presence in Kenya has earned her a local name, Nga Musyoki[47]. Michelle loves not just the country of Kenya but especially the people of Kenya. She is not one to get too much involved in teaching or telling the kids what to do during TUBE. Instead, she takes time to just be with them, listen to their life stories and only offers words of wisdom and encouragement as appropriate. It is amazing how much one can accomplish just by being present. Listening actively is important because it communicates to the other person that they do matter. Because of her genuine caring, Michelle has touched the lives of many kids in very special ways.

You see, by God's grace, Christians have been given what it takes to completely turn the dark world into a marvelous light. These kids have known nothing but darkness. Disease has come at night and snatched their parents away like a thief. In John 10:10 Jesus said, "The thief's purpose is to steal and kill and to destroy. My purpose is to give them a rich and satisfying life." (NLT) As opposed to a thief or hireling, Jesus is a devoted shepherd who went as far as laying his life down for his sheep—his Church. As followers of Jesus Christ, we are called to come alongside the millions of forgotten orphans and extend a little bit of what Jesus has given us.

Stanley M. Mutunga

Chapter 5:

Education:
How Important is It?

"Mutish"

"I knew that I wasn't born to fail but I didn't know how the script would go. I had no hope. I thought I had been forgotten... I now have hope and in my mind's eye I can see far. Tumaini has not only met my material needs but has really inspired me." ~Mutish

Mutish is a confident and ambitious 21-year-old man. He graduated at the top of all Tumaini kids who graduated from high school in the December 2006 class. His dream in life was to become a missionary doctor, but when he lost his parents, he thought those dreams were doomed. From a very young age, he was moved from home to home and when he was in the ninth grade, he dropped out due to lack of school fees. That is when Diamond Canyon Christian Church (in California) stepped in and provided sponsorship. Mutish confesses that without education, he "*…could have been one of the thugs in town."* He remembers a time when he had *"no home, no food, and no hope but now I have Jesus and all else I need."* An ever smiling, charming and joyous individual, Mutish is looking forward to be used by the Lord to help heal others. He adds, *"Tumaini has profoundly touched my life."*

Today, Mutish is living his dream. He has joined a Catholic seminary in Nairobi to commence his studies in Theology and Medicine. He will then proceed to Spain for further studies before he comes back to serve his people. Who knows how many lives Mutish will end up touching!

"Mo"

Mo is a vivacious 19-year-old woman. Always dreaming and reaching for the stars, she is ever thankful for the chance to study. She and her elder brother were orphaned at very early ages and left under the care of a grandmother who couldn't educate them. Through child sponsorship, Mo has been given a chance to excel. Already she has been accepted at the university to study Food Science and Nutrition. During her spare time, she hopes to complete accountancy courses towards her CPA certificate. I can't even begin to imagine the many lives that this young woman will touch in the years to come. What a hope she has received!

"Cox"

An only child, Cox lost his parents when he was very young. An incredibly brilliant 21- year-old man, Cox is living his dream. When I asked him about the one thing that sponsorship has brought him, he did not mince words: "*I have found hope in Jesus. With the education I am receiving, I can see the light at the end of the tunnel. Hope for a boy who was otherwise lost and forgotten. Education has also brought me peace."* Cox is a multi-talented young man—very active in church as a musician and in the civic life of his town. He is starting his university studies in the fall of 2010 to major in Economics and Statistics. The sky is the limit of what this eight-cylinder kind of a guy will do in the future. Already touching lives by counseling younger AIDS orphans, Cox has the potential of touching many, many, lives in the future.

"John"

I introduced you to John earlier. He is a quiet, 21-year-old young man. With inquisitive eyes and a gracious personality, he is the persona of grace and peace, very humble and focused. I asked him what education had meant for him thus far. His response: *"Hope is the word that comes to mind. In particular, I have been offered an opportunity to know and grow in the Lord as well as a rare chance to pursue quality education. These two gives me hope that I otherwise could only dream of prior to sponsorship."* A sophomore in college, John is looking forward to the future: *"I want to share this hope with other needy kids in the future. I know there are other children out there who are in the same situation I was before Tumaini came in and I want to be someone who will help such children and give them hope for their future as I have been given."*

John is not only one of the brightest students sponsored by Tumaini, but also one of the top students in the nation in his chosen field of study. As a sophomore completing a degree in Finance, he is also working on the final stages of a rigorous CPA program. With his mental brilliance, humble demeanor and love for the Lord, I can't wait to see where the Lord will place him and the number of lives he will touch.

I can go on and on! There are so many kids I have met through this ministry whose lives have taken a 180-degree turn for the better, but I cannot list them all here.

Just a Dollar a Day!

The one factor in the educational success in the stories of Mutish, Cox, Mo and John is that it only cost $1.00 a day to help them realize their dreams! Yes, a dollar a day! I don't know about you but to think that a decision made by a church in one corner of the world to spare a dollar a day has turned a potential 'town thug' into a missionary doctor is more than mind boggling to me. To think that a decision made by an individual thousands of miles away to spare a dollar a day has turned a herds boy into a potential world renowned financial expert who has the ethical background to influence the world markets positively, this is a blessing beyond description.

When the Tumaini or Community Transformers children write letters to their sponsors, one of the main points they talk about is their education. In fact, many times that is the only subject they write about. Most children in Kenya and their families believe that the only way to get out of the poverty cycle is through education and they have proof of it. They have seen that in a country where unemployment hovers between 40% and 60%, the few who have made it are college graduates and those in the business community. But they also know that, even to get into the business world, they will need capital and an education. To acquire an education, many poor families will spare no expense including selling their only investment, land, to ensure that their children get some education.

My Story

I give God the glory for who I am today. Without knowing Jesus at an early age, I honestly don't think I would be alive today. I do know that without my education, I would not be writing this book. Being the last born in a family of ten, I grew up in a very poor family and my education was the last thing on my parents' mind. They themselves didn't have any formal education and school came a distant second to taking care of the few animals they owned and working on the family farm whenever there were rains. My father's view was that school will always be there but rains came and went. Consequently, during the rainy months, I missed a lot of school sessions during my elementary and high school years. Still, I was determined—those who knew me then will tell you that I was a resilient kid. When one of my elder brothers, for example, dropped from high school in his sophomore year due to lack of fees and tuition, I decided to stay on. I did all kinds of manual jobs, going from town to town on market days trading in goats and cows, burning charcoal—to pay for my education. To cut the long story short, I knew education was important and nothing was going to stop me as long as I had breath.

In looking back, I believe I have been able to travel and network with global Christians about the plight of AIDS orphans partly because of my own education. By God's grace, I am able to relate to and articulate the needs of millions of forgotten AIDS orphans and widows across the globe.

Education and Economic Development

Education is intricately related to a nation's development. Any nation that wants to grow and sustain itself must have a critical mass of educated professionals to lead the various development sectors of the nation. As already indicated, sub-Saharan Africa is the least developed region of the world. I believe that the children we are assisting now will be part of the economic solution for Africa. These children need not only an enduring relationship with Jesus but also the best education that the world can offer. These youngsters need adequate training so that they can transform the region in both the physical and spiritual arenas. Africa needs many more Mutish's, Mo's, Cox's and John's in order to move forward. Just from these few individuals, we are potentially looking at a food and nutrition expert, a medical doctor and two financial experts. Africa, a continent with almost one billion people, now needs more of these Christian professionals. What an opportunity for the Church to make a difference.

The relationship between quality education and economic development has been well documented. Meeting in Johannesburg, South Africa in 2002, *World Summit on Sustainable Development* in collaboration with UNESCO came up with what they saw as five core characteristics of education for sustainable development:

- Envisioning: Being able to imagine a better future. The premise is that if we know where we want to go, we will be better able to work out how to get there.

- Critical thinking and reflection: Learning to question our current belief systems and to recognize the assumptions underlying our knowledge, perspective and opinions. Critical thinking skills help people learn to examine economic, environmental, social and cultural structures in the context of sustainable development.

- Systemic thinking: Acknowledging complexities and looking for links and synergies when trying to find solutions to problems.

- Building partnerships: Promoting dialogue and negotiation, learning to work together.

- Participation in decision-making: Empowering people. [48]

These five characteristics are by no means exhaustive but represent a good starting place. The point here is the critical importance of education. Only quality education will help orphans provide for themselves and their own families and also serve as a knowledge base for what is needed to move a nation and a continent ahead economically. Educating people at the international level will uplift the economic standards of their vairous nations, of the continent and indeed, the entire world.

I think it is those who have suffered the most who are best able to relate to the needs of other forgotten populations. Therefore I am convinced that it is these formerly forgotten children who will make the best missionary doctors, nutrionists, accountants and ethical financial planners and it is they who will save the world from the next economic downturn such as we have witnessed over the past few years. It is these folks who will make the best preachers, teachers, farmers, professors, fathers, husbands, wives, politicians, journalists and the like. In all these areas, education plays a critical role.

Walter W. McMahon, a Professor of Economics and Education who has worked in Europe, America, Asia and the Middle East, has researched and written an important work [49] in which he ably ties economic development to education. In a nutshell, he argues that education is the key for knowledge-based global economies. The argument is that economies depend on education not only for the diffusion of knowledge and learning new techniques, but also for long-term poverty reduction and improved heath. There is very little debate that much of the economic development around the globe is driven by folks who have been well schooled in various economic principles and policies. Coincidentally, I am writing this book at a time when the economy has tumbled almost globally. Who did the American President, Barak Obama, turn to when he needed to lead the nation's economic recovery? The experts. He sought out well-known, credible economic gurus to advise him on how to lead the nation back to its financial stability. Such a knowledge base is needed across the globe.

Meet the Amazing Biko

The story of Biko comes to mind when I think of the critical role that basic knowledge can play in the life of a young man trying to figure out life's challenges. "Biko" is a 22- year-old Tumaini sponsored young man who lost his father at the age of 16. He comes from a large family and has nine siblings: 6 sisters and 3 brothers. When their father died, they were left in the sole care of their mother, a peasant woman with no formal education. With so many mouths to feed, she did all she could to take care of her children. Though she had every intention to educate her children, most of them had to drop from school for lack of tuition and fees. Biko went to work for the local merchants until he was sponsored by Tumaini. He has since completed high school (the only one to complete high school in his family) and is waiting to join college and train as an accountant.

A couple of years ago, a very unfortunate incident happened that pitted Biko against his mother and the local government officials. Basically, someone had tried to defraud his mother of a portion of their land, their only investment. Unaware that it was a fraudulent scheme, Biko's mother seemed to go along with the plan since she needed to put food on the table. However, when Biko found out about the plan, he refused to go along with it and a bitter wrangle erupted between him, his mother and the corrupt system that was aimed at taking their land. Biko stood his ground and went to court to defend the family land.

Narrating the story, Biko told me that this was the most trying time of his young life. As he said, *"You see, since I became a Christian and began to know the truth, I have become very bold. When I decided to take this case and fight for my family, I knew it would be an uphill task. I didn't have money to hire a lawyer. My mom didn't know she was being lied to.*

Some of the local officials were colluding with the illegal buyer to defraud us. I made sure that every time I went to court I was in my school uniform and bare feet. I wanted the judge and the jurors to see the innocence of a schoolboy who was doing nothing but fighting for his and his sibling's rights. I prayed in preparation of each court appearance and read any book I could find relative to the land laws in Kenya. At the end of the day, I won the case."

As I listened to Biko animatedly tell the story, I could not help but think, *Wow, how many 17-year-old kids have the knowledge, the courage, and the audacity to pull off something like this!* I am sure there are many factors that account for the bravery of Biko. Both nature and nurture can be thanked for his faith, natural abilities, talents and temperament, but I clearly see the role of his education which gave him the confidence to confront the corrupt system that was out to take away the family's only investment.

HIV/AIDS and Education

In a region where women still don't hold much power, education is the one tool that effectively offers them some control over their bodies. Education certainly provides women an academic foundation for acquiring good jobs, but it also offers them knowledge about their civil rights as well as accurate information about preventing diseases and especially the transmission of the HIV virus. Education gives women social and economic power so that they won't have to rely on unscrupulous men masquerading as 'rescuers' who are only out to destroy their future. More and more we are seeing young women like Mo rise above the male chauvinism that traditionally thwarts the dreams of so many young women. Why? Obviously knowing Christ as their savior has been essential to their success and strength so far but I would add that being well-educated women has played a significant role.

A report put together by *World Food Program* (WFP) suggests a direct correlation between the prevalence of HIV/AIDS and levels of education obtained. The report covers several sub-Saharan countries and is especially poignant as it sheds important light on the effects on women. A few examples will suffice:

- *A Zambian study showed that HIV/AIDS spreads twice as fast among uneducated girls (Vandemoortele & Delamonica, 2000)*

- *Another Zambian study found a marked decline in HIV prevalence rates in 15-19 year-old boys and girls with medium to higher education level but an increase in lower education levels (Kelly, 2000)*

- *Young rural Ugandans with secondary education were three times less likely than those with no education to be HIV positive (De Walque, 2004)*

- *A Kenyan study found that girls who stayed in school were four times more likely to remain virgins than those who dropped out (UNICEF, 2002)*

- *In Zimbabwe, secondary education had a protective effect against HIV for women that lasted to adulthood. Girls aged 15-18 who had dropped out of school were six times more likely to be HIV positive than those who were still enrolled (Gregson, Waddell, and Chandiwana, 2001)* [50]

These statistics clearly speak for themselves. Education plays a critical role in so many aspects of life for the sector of the population under study. For AIDS- orphaned children, particularly girls, they are even more vulnerable compared to those with parents. One could argue that they are doubly vulnerable and therefore in many cases, obtaining a formal education becomes the most significant and effective way out of this vicious circle of ignorance, disease and death.

For me personally, educating girls and young women such as Monique, Liz, Mo, and Grace is not simply a statistical affair; I believe that we are changing the world by empowering more women through education. By educating young men such as John, Mutish, Cox, and Joey, we are not only changing the fortunes of otherwise forgotten children but we are changing the world through education. These men and women love the Lord and their sense of service will be contagious to their communities, and the rest of the country, continent, and indeed, the world.

Closer to Home

My own anecdotal research in our organization indicates that level of education has played a big role in the spread of HIV/AIDS. For example, about 50% of the AIDS orphans that we sponsor through Tumaini come from single mothers who had little or no secondary education. A great many of these women were minimally employed in socially lower-end jobs in large towns, and prone to getting involved in riskier sexual encounters with multiple partners in order to augment their all too meager income. Others were simply ignorant of the various methods through which HIV is spread and engaged in risky behaviors that led them to contract the deadly disease.

Given these facts and the case studies I've shared, it would seem to me that one sure way of preventing another generation of HIV victims is through education. By God's grace, the solution is in our hands. We simply cannot afford to forget another generation of young girls and boys or stand on the sidelines and watch as they grow up without Jesus, without education, without hope and walk right into the arms of death. We cannot afford to wait for another year. We cannot afford to wait another day. No, we must act today.

> *"My people are destroyed for lack of knowledge. Because you have rejected knowledge, I will also reject you from being a priest for Me. Because you have forgotten the law of your God I also will forget your children." (Hosea 4:6 NKJV)*

This verse comes in the middle of a long and stern statement to the people of God. Beginning in Hosea chapter 4 verse 1, the people of God are accused of being untrustworthy and unfaithful to God's statutes. They are accused of lacking kindness and compassion toward the poor and the downtrodden. They are accused of lacking knowledge of God. It is important to pay attention to the larger context and point out that, the knowledge that the people of God are lacking here is not of statistics or accountancy or even medicine. The knowledge they lack is that of practicing the truth. In other words, the focus is not so much on *not knowing* God's truth, but more so in *not practicing* it.

For us today, I see at least two ways of applying this passage. First, it is a call to us as the Church to practice the truth as we know it. The biblical call for Christians is to respond tangibly to the needs of the poor is well documented. When it comes to the needs of the HIV/AIDS victims and the havoc the disease has caused, we already know enough if we want to make a difference. As we saw in an earlier chapter, the number of victims of this pandemic is staggering.

Second, by implication, there is a call in this passage for the need to educate the poor. By education, I am not referring simply to diplomas and degrees. These are important, but there are other aspects of education that are equally important. We need to address the educational needs of these forgotten children and widows in holistic ways so that they not only have the necessary skills to function competently in a 21st century world, but also know the Lord and live in fullness and hope. Truly, people do perish for lack of knowledge.

Stanley M. Mutunga

Chapter 6

Hunger:
When One Meal a Day
is Luxury

"Milcah"

Let me introduce you to two very special women that I have met over the past couple of years, Milcah and Teca. Before I met them, I thought I knew a thing or two about hunger. No- I did not.

Milcah is an 82-year-old grandmother who lives under very poor conditions. A widow, Milcah had six children: two sons and four daughters. One of her sons and three of her daughters have died from AIDS, leaving her with 11 orphan grandchildren to take care of. In total, Milcah has 43 grandchildren and 36 great-grandchildren. Of the 11 orphan grandchildren, 8 were already sponsored through Tumaini when I first visited her humble home. The morning I visited, one of the 3 unsponsored children had been sent home from pre-school because Milcah could not afford to pay his $5.00 semester fee! I am glad to report that the other three children have since been sponsored, which has greatly lifted her burden. Milcah recalled the days she and her family used to have only one meal a day. Despite her situation, she was grateful because, as she put it, *"We are well off compared to some of my neighbors."*

In my travels among the poor—both in the rural areas and in the slums of Africa, the one statement I hear often is what Milcah said: *we are well off compared to some of my neighbors.* And yet some of the people who utter these statements barely have enough to have a single decent meal a day! Where does such deep-seated gratitude in the face of abject poverty come from?

The two fresh burial sites on Milcah's compound are a stark reminder of the havoc that AIDS had caused in her home. Four adult children had been buried just outside her dilapidated mud houses next to each other. Gazing on the skies and reflecting on the loss of her kids, Milcah still thanked God for his goodness. I knew right there and then sitting next to me was a woman whose faith in God could only be explained in mystical terms. She compares her loss with that of the biblical Job. *"I have lost so much,"* she said, quickly adding that her life was in God's hands. *"I have faith in God and really have nothing to worry about,"* she quipped. As I looked at the glow on her face, I admired her faith. Her demeanor reminded me of a statement by C.S. Lewis years ago when he observed that *"God whispers to us in our pleasure, speaks in our conscience, but shouts in our pains: it is his megaphone to rouse a deaf world."* [51] There was no doubt how clearly God had spoken in the heart of this woman through pain that most of us can only imagine. By extension, God used the pain that Milcah had experienced to somehow touch my own heart. I always find it hard to articulate but it seems to me that when we are open to God's inner working in our lives, he has a way of using others' situations to speak to our deepest senses and feelings.

Even after a year whenever I think of Milcah I ask myself, could anyone not be touched by this woman's situation? I am not talking about pity. Milcah has experienced a lot of pain, but the last thing she needs is pity. Given her faith and hope in God and her resilience, Milcah needs someone to come alongside and give her a hand-up. For example, Milcah does not need someone to build her a mansion but to repair her mud huts. I left her home thinking to myself, how can I as an arm of the Church come alongside her and be a part of the solution to help meet her needs?

Although there was abject poverty at that home, what challenged me the most was Milcah's faith and her joyful demeanor in the face of such horrible circumstances. My reaction surprised me because I grew up in poverty and I know what poverty is first hand. I know what it means to have one meal a day. But at least, I had both parents and even though we were near the bottom of the pile in poverty, we had each other. Milcah's situation is, however, worse by comparison. At her age, she is carrying a heavy burden, taking care of 11 orphans.

Let me be clear here.

I do not question the sincerity of Milcah's faith in God. In fact, many of us who have so much in material wealth can learn a lot about contentment just by spending one morning with Milcah. Despite her undeniable poverty, she is one of the happiest people that I have ever met. She is also one of the most contented Christians I have met. It is such encounters that not only challenge my faith, but gives me the zeal to keep going. I continue to be grateful to God for the opportunity that he has given me as a Christian to respond to the needs of so many of God's children in dire need.

Despite Milcah's contentment, however, I could not help but think of her immediate needs. Milcah's is one of the few homes that I have visited and found myself shedding tears. I found myself asking the question, why would this devout child of God face so much hunger in a world that has so much? I did what I could to put food on the table for about a week. As I left her compound, the faces of those beautiful children were etched in my mind's eye. I wondered, *what about their future?* I thanked God that by his grace, at least this one family was connected with people of faith who can help. Otherwise, these children would have fallen into the cracks and become mere statistics.

"Teca"

Teca is a 36-year-old single mother of two and stepmother of five. She lives in Mathare slums in Nairobi where she and her seven kids call home. In a way, her life story is so familiar given the life in the slums. Yet it is unique in many aspects. Having no education and no resources, Teca got married early in her teens. Unfortunately, she contracted HIV and when she developed full-blown AIDS, she was abandoned by her husband and family with no job and no food to feed herself and the seven kids under her care. Indeed, most of her friends abandoned her when it became apparent that it was a matter of time before she would succumb to AIDS and die. But even in her darkest hour, a precious few of her neighbors remained close and helped her with some food and anti-retroviral drugs to keep her going, if just for a few more days. However, it reached a point when she knew her death was eminent and from that day on she refused to continue taking medicine.

She reasoned that in death, she would cease to be a burden to her few friends. Her greatest fear, however, was what would happen to her seven children. What would they eat? Who will take care of them? How would her children afford to go to school? Will they join other homeless kids in the slum, get involved in all manner of social ills, die young and simply become statistics? Those questions weighed heavily on Teca as she lay on a thin mattress tucked at the corner of the mud floor waiting to die. I still remember her emphatic words when she narrated this sad story to me. She put it this way at an interview: *"I so much wanted to die and forget everything about life."* In the slum, a sea of hopelessness where everyone is struggling to survive, she believed that no one would think of taking on someone else's burden.

It was during this darkest hour that one of the few remaining friends told her about a Christian agency called HEART (Health Education for Africa Resource Teams) and offered to tell them about her dire situation.

Teca was not sure if she should bother them since she was inevitably going to die soon. HEART staff visited her one morning in her dark and crowded shack. They brought some basic supplies and encouraged her to take food and the anti-retroviral medicine. After much persuasion, she agreed to give life another chance. Through this intervention, Teca not only got food and medicine but HEART, through its Women's Empowerment Equality Project (WEEP) program offered to help her get a skill. WEEP is an arm of HEART through which HIV/AIDS positive mothers are helped with nutrition and medicines to stay alive, and they are trained in a marketable trade skill so that they can earn a living and provide for their families. Teca was offered a chance to train as a seamstress so that she can support her family. As she was just getting off the ground, Teca developed some gynecological complications. Again, HEART assisted with two operations to correct the situation.

Today, whenever Teca talks about HEART, her face beams with a big smile and she is full of life. I have had a chance to interview Teca twice now. As I have gotten to know her better, I see how God put a chain of people in her life- first her few friends and then HEART- and how much she has changed spiritually, emotionally and even physically within a matter of a year. I think it is exactly these kinds of friends that Henri Nouwen had in mind when he wrote these words: *"The friend who can be silent with us in a moment of despair and confusion, who can stay with us in a hour of grief and bereavement, who can tolerate not-knowing, not curing, not healing, and face with us the reality of our powerlessness, that is the friend who cares."*[52]

It has been two years since Teca crossed paths with such friends including HEART. Today, Teca is happy and strong, and she is working everyday to provide for her seven children. By her own admission, of all the women that HEART has assisted, she has benefited the most from this partnership. By all accounts, she was the sickest of all the WEEP women and the fact that she is still alive today and thriving is a miracle in itself. Meeting and talking with Teca, one cannot help but witness how she initially depended on HEART for all her needs. But with just a little hand-up, she is now able to meet most of her basic needs. Getting her health back has been the key. Today she feels that she has been given her life back, literally and figuratively speaking.

To think that for every Milcah, there are millions of other Milcah's who live unnoticed in the rural areas of Africa, SE Asia, Mexico and South America is a challenge to the world. To think that for every Teca, there are millions of other Teca's who live unnoticed in the slums of African cities, Mexican cities, SE Asia cities, Indian cities and South American cities is a challenge to the world. It is a shame that in the 21st century, at a time when the globe has been connected more than at any other time in the history of the world through technology we could still be talking about 1 billion hungry people.

For the remainder of this chapter, I will address several salient points: the disconnect that is leading to hunger; a reality check on the world's priorities; the scope of poverty; how bureaucracy hampers charity work; and finally, the Church's mandate in tackling hunger.

Why the Disconnect?

The level of poverty that these two women and their families have had to deal with brings tears to many who have met them. Unfortunately, there are millions of grandmothers and young AIDS widows in sub-Saharan Africa and other parts of the world whose stories have turned out for the worse. There are millions of Milcah's and Teca's who are forgotten and the world will never know a thing about them except the statistics. Why should this be so in a world that is full of resources and better connected than any other time in history? Why should the world watch silently while so many people suffer with the needed resources literally around the corner from them? Why is it that while we live in a so-called flat world and global village, we seem to be either unable or unwilling to rush those resources to the rescue of the world's poor? Why is there such a disconnect between the people on the bottom of the pile and the non-poor?

I will not pretend to know all the reasons why the political powers, the G8's of the world, the G20's of the world, and so forth-- why they don't rally and eradicate hunger, place it at a higher priority. If there really is a concerted effort underway by these great world powers to end hunger, the needle moves too slowly for those in the trenches, like Milcah and Teca, to notice. I am aware that the year 2015 is a target year for the U.N.

to eradicate extreme poverty, along with the other seven global problems they are trying to address. Frankly, I am not optimistic that they will meet the goal. I do, however, feel that there is even a more serious disconnect. I am talking about the church of Jesus Christ. I am not even sure how to define this disconnect. Sometimes I wonder if the non-poor in the Church are unaware of the level of hunger that their brothers and sisters in some corners of the world have to endure. Is it a theological disconnect? Still, could it be a philosophical issue?

Theologians, philosophers and historians, among others, have wrestled with the question of God's love vis-à-vis the suffering in the world, including suffering from hunger. I still remember many years ago in college sitting in a philosophy of religion class discussing the issue of a theodicy—the idea of a loving God who allows the suffering of so many in his beloved creation. I still remember how the answers to that old question were framed depending on one's theological position, with the more conservative, reformed groups tucked in one corner while those who pushed for a strong choice and human freedom stood on the other.

Whatever the reason is, there is an apparent disconnect between the suffering in the world and the Sunday morning worship services in well air-conditioned places of worship. And I am not talking about posh churches in the west only. There are mega churches in Africa as well. Yes, the Bible tells us that the 'poor will always be with us' so I have no illusions of completely eradicating poverty. Still doesn't the fact that both the Old Testament and the New Testament call for compassion on the poor suggest that we should at least do something to mitigate poverty?

In the real world we do not have the luxury of that kind of armchair theologizing. We are dealing with real life situations here. As a Christian, I believe every generation in every place must re-ask the question, listen to the Holy Spirit's voice and respond accordingly. If it is true that HIV/AIDS is the greatest humanitarian disaster of the 21st century, Christians have no luxury to either stand on the fence or look the other way. We must get involved. I liked how the young pastor of a mega church put the situation recently. About the aftermath of AIDS he said, "... *how the Church responds to the HIV/AIDS pandemic is a significant call that God has placed on our generation.*"[53] We must do our part to address the global poverty that is being exacerbated by this deadly disease. We must quit theologizing or philosophizing about world hunger and get our hands dirty actually dealing with it. I am not talking about emotional exuberance but thoughtful and carefully planned involvement with the hungry and hurting people of the world. Given the many calls for the resources that God has entrusted to us, we must ask ourselves serious questions about stewardship and act accordingly. Standing on the sidelines, however, is not an option. The Bible says that where our treasure is, there our hearts will be also (Mat. 6:21).

A Reality Check

As I write this chapter, the world is celebrating 40 years since astronauts Neil Armstrong and Buzz Aldrin stepped on the moon on July 20, 1969. I was not one of the 500 million people who watched the event live on TV sets across the globe then. Actually, I didn't even know how to spell the word TV at the time. I was a simple herd's boy in the villages of SE Kenya. There was only one old transistor radio in the entire village of 3,000 people and there was a buzz about something important happening somewhere on the globe. I knew that something important was happening somehow connecting the Americans and the moon. That was the extent of my space program knowledge at the time.

Today, NASA and other interested parties are calling for trips back to the moon as a launching pad to visit Mars. Estimates indicate that the price tag is going to be much higher than what it cost to go to the moon 40 years ago. At that time, the United States spent $25.4 billion on the Apollo space program, which translates to nearly $150 billion in current dollars. It is said that going to Mars would even cost more. I found it rather telling what astronaut Buzz Aldrin said when asked about his experience on the moon. He put it this way, *"This is a very desolate place…It's just boring. It's all one color that varies depending on the sun angle. But the sky is black; it's all black except the one object there, the Earth, and the object behind us, the sun."*[54] I don't know about you but I find *desolate, boring, all one color, black* descriptive of a depressing place to be. Did you notice that the only two objects they found interesting were the earth where we live and the sun, which provides energy that we need! Sometimes I wonder whether we as human beings have misplaced our priorities. Would it not make more sense to do all that we can to make life for people on planet earth better before we can spend insane amounts of money on other planets that are not even interesting to the astronauts?

Reading my critique above, one would think that I harbor ill will for the space program. The truth is, I do not. I am actually pro-space program and other scientific discoveries that would help address the challenges here on earth. I am only using this as an example of a costly program that, while it may have some future potential benefits, it is taking away from today's very real needs. Simply put, too much resource is diverted to 'things' when human beings are suffering from disease and hunger. This should raise an important question about us as the human species.

The concern I have about luxurious scientific programs also goes for the untold sums of money that developing countries spend on building armies while the populace suffers inhumane levels of poverty. *The International Action Network on Small Arms* (IANSA) for example paints a very telling picture of how billions of dollars were squandered in Africa in the recent past for on-going wars on the continent.[55] The report states that even without the human tragedy, armed conflict costs Africa around $18 billion per year.[56]

I found the following report very disturbing:*" Around $300bn since 1990 has been lost by Algeria, Angola, Burundi, Central African Republic, Chad, Democratic Republic of Congo (DRC), Republic of Congo, Côte d'Ivoire, Djibouti, Eritrea, Ethiopia, Ghana, Guinea, Guinea-Bissau, Liberia, Niger, Nigeria, Rwanda, Senegal, Sierra Leone, South Africa, Sudan and Uganda. ...If this money was not lost due to armed conflict, it could solve the problems of HIV and AIDS in Africa, or it could address Africa's needs in education, clean water and sanitation, and prevent tuberculosis and malaria"[57]*.

This is not another call to equal redistribution of global resources. I have heard the argument that the US, which comprises only 6% of the world population but consumes 40% of world resources, should re-distribute to the have-nots. Actually, that would be irresponsible considering that some countries have gotten to the level of poverty they are in because of bad governance, among other reasons. I am not so naïve to ignore the world's political and economic policies. I am quite aware that political institutions are about self-preservation and every country takes actions that are deemed best for the welfare and interests of its citizenry and self-enhancement. This is not even about a call to socialism either.

Rather, I am only calling the Church to be fully aware of global events and how they conspire intentionally or otherwise to make the lives of the hungry miserable. Some in the Church have positions of power to prophetically challenge the nations, but most of us are simply called to be the salt and light in an otherwise dark world. As the Suffi story reminded us, since it is our nature to do good, then we should not allow the events in our world to change our nature to do good. I want Christians to see how millions of orphans and their families have been forgotten by a world that is too busy with other priorities. I am calling upon Christians to remember that these are not just interesting statistics but they each represent real human beings who are going hungry and suffering from diseases, many of which can be prevented and eliminated at twelve cents each!

The Scope of Poverty

The question of how to measure poverty has been of much debate. World Bank, for example, defines poverty in very practical terms: *"Poverty is hunger. Poverty is lack of shelter. Poverty is being sick and not being able to see a doctor. Poverty is not having access to school and not knowing how to read. Poverty is not having a job, is fear for the future, living one day at a time. Poverty is losing a child to illness brought about by unclean water. Poverty is powerlessness, lack of representation and freedom".*[58]

A cursory survey of world affairs would indicate that poverty levels are not going down but instead, the numbers keep rising. Indeed, the estimates are staggering. World Bank estimated that in 2008 some 1.4 billion people globally still lived below the poverty line measured at $1.25 and $2.00 day.[59] As we already saw, sub-Saharan Africa is at the bottom of the pile when it comes to poverty. In Kenya, for example, 46% of the population lives on under a $1.00 a day and unemployment fluctuates between 40% and 60%.

The World Bank report is collaborated by U.N. reports as well. According to a U.N. report, for the first time in recorded history world hunger has reached the 1 billion people mark.[60] The report went on to add, *"Almost all the worlds undernourished live in developing countries, where food prices have fallen more slowly than in the richer nations... Poor countries need more aid and agricultural investment to cope".* [61] Predictably, the report adds, *"Sub-Saharan Africa has the highest rate of hunger, with 265 million undernourished representing 32 percent of the region's population."*[62]

Paul Collier, Professor of Economics and Director of the Center for the Study of African Economics at Oxford University, corroborates the above report, stating that there are *"1 billion poor who are falling behind and falling apart while the rest of the world continues to advance.*[63]*"* He then articulates four traps that have kept this billion at the bottom. These traps include: the conflict trap, the natural resources trap, the trap of being landlocked with bad neighbors and the trap of bad governance in a small country.[64] According to Collier, 70% of these 1 billion people live in 58 countries in Africa.[65]

In the same vein, Gregory Clark, Economics Professor at the University of California, Davis, makes a very interesting claim. Based on his study on the history of quantitative economics, he suggests that some countries would be better off had the Industrial Revolution not interfered with their progress. He says, *"Countries such as Malawi or Tanzania would be better off in material terms had they never had contact with the industrialized world and instead continued in their pre-industrial state".*[66] There is really no way of ever testing Clark's theory, but the reality on the ground in respect to the two countries and others in sub-Saharan Africa makes one wonder if there isn't some merit in the professor's assessment. What I found even more poignant is the next point he makes: *"The gap in incomes between countries is of the order of 50:1. There walk the earth now both the richest people who ever lived and the poorest."*[67] Wow! This is 21st century?

An aspect of poverty that is especially disturbing is the number of children who die every year from preventable diseases. The U.N. children's agency, UNICEF, reports that 1.4 million children die each year from diseases that could be prevented by vaccination. [68] William Easterly, himself a one-time employee of World Bank, laments the fact that global society can get entertainment to rich adults and children in real time while it can't get twelve cent medicine to dying, poor children.[69]

Jeffrey Sachs paints a more optimistic picture. In a widely read book, Sachs argues that some good has been accomplished by the global community to mitigate poverty and that we should build on the good done.[70] Sachs is bold enough to even make recommendations on how rich nations can help *eradicate* poverty. I don't think poverty eradication is theologically defensible but I know the Church can do a great deal in terms of reducing poverty.

Whether one agrees with Easterly's view that, for 50 years the West has accomplished nothing with the 2.3 trillion dollars already spend by U.N. and its financial institutions to address poverty; or Sachs' view that something has actually been accomplished and that optimism is needed to finally eradicate poverty; or even Collier's middle of the ground position that 5 billion people are out of poverty and that the West should now focus on the remaining billion (mostly in Africa) and get the job done, the issue has been very well articulated. The fact is, there are still at least one billion people who are at the bottom of the pile. There are still one billion people who are loved by God who have little or nothing to eat. Some of these are the forgotten AIDS orphans. Milcah and Teca and their families are a microcosm of these one billion souls. It has been said often that statistics do not bleed, but humans do. These lovely ladies are not just statistics; they are real people who give a face to what can otherwise be a very dry academic discussion.

These statistics bother me. I know there is a lot of blame to go around. Let me be clear about one important point. I believe that there are certain things only governments can do. Governments have the responsibility of good rule—which includes making laws and enforcing them. Governments are responsible for putting up infrastructure and other important networks to enable its citizens to carry out its affairs. For example, it is the responsibility of governments to construct roads, sink bore holes for water, and provide access to food and security for its citizens, among other services. As a Christian, I know that God sets up government institutions and gives them the responsibility to take care of its citizenry. However, since man decried theocracy (God's rule) in favor of kingdoms (including democracy) when they said to Samuel, *"Give us a king to judge us like all the other nations have,"* (1 Sam 8:5, NLT) things went haywire with the rich getting richer and the poor getting poorer. I know that governments of the poorest of the poor countries have contributed to the sorry situations in which their citizens find themselves in. There is no excuse for this state of situation.

What I am calling for, however, is the Church to realize that she has always had a role in God's running of his affairs. Even during theocratic rule, God reminded the non-poor to come to the aid of the poor, the orphan, the widow, and the alien in times of need. *"The poor will always be with you,"* Moses reminded the Israelites in Deut. 15:11. When we live in a world where there is a discrepancy between the world we live in and world the poor live in, is it not part of Christian duty to respond to these needs as we are able to?

I have seen how Christian agencies, particularly the ones that take what William Easterly has called a *searcher* mentality, make a difference in the lives of the poor in real time. Milcah and Teca are classic case studies. I want the world to know that the poor, especially the AIDS victims and their families, should not be blamed for their poverty because they are truly victims of myriads of factors—corruption, poor planning, disease, environmental factors, among others. This is really an opportunity for the Church to serve as the very hands and feet of Jesus Christ.

Charity Without Bureaucracy

In the spring of 2008, I was watching a news bulletin one evening on TV in Kenya. That particular evening, they highlighted on the devastation that had been brought about by a three-year drought in the country and how that had compounded the famine across Kenya. They featured two parts of the country where the people ran out of food and they had resorted to some very unconventional ways of feeding their families. In one District, people had resorted to eating whatever wild roots they could find in the land. In another District, families were boiling unripe mangoes for breakfast, lunch and dinner. I must say that as poor as I may have been growing up, I never had to rely on wild roots or unripe mangoes for all my meals a day. I was moved by the plight of those families to tears. The fact that this was happening on the heels of post-election violence in Kenya bothered me even more. To see leaders focused on their political survival and pay little attention to the starving population did not endear me to what the government stood for. But I knew as a Christian I could not just flip the channels and move to the next soap opera for mindless entertainment. I knew that beyond giving whatever monies I had to help a few families, God had placed me in a position to respond more widely.

A few weeks later, I sent out a letter to my network of Christian friends. Here is an excerpt: "*When I was in Kenya in January, a government report was released to the effect that some 10 million Kenyans were facing starvation this year. Folks, 10 million are a third of the entire population of Kenya! One question that people ask me is 'why?' Why are so many people in Kenya facing starvation? I really don't have a good answer to that question. Maybe a combination of several factors…three long years of drought… inept and corrupt government officials…poor planning…lack of modern agricultural technology? I don't know. The list can be long and daunting.*

What I do know, however, is that there are innocent people facing starvation in Kenya today. As a Christian I am called to act responsibly as God's hands and feet in this matter. As Christians, we know what God wants us to do in these matters.

Because the situation has been exacerbated by the ongoing famine I am coming to you for a special donation… Fully aware of our economic situation in our country, I am asking those who can to seriously consider giving a one time gift to this emergency food fund."[71]

I included some suggested giving amounts directly related to the cost of staple foods and how many families each amount would actually assist. The response was immediate and I am touched by the generosity of these Christians. These friends are not millionaires (at least not that I am aware of) but these folks have big hearts. One hundred percent of the funds given went straight to the people who needed it most, and I am pleased to report that we were able to reach these most needy in time. We literally prevented families from starving to death!

Here is my point. People still care. However, many times they are skeptical about whether their funds will reach the intended poor either because of bureaucracy or corruption or a combination of both. Other times, people don't know how or who to channel their help through. At least in this one point I agree with William Easterly: Searchers get the job done! There is no good reason over a billion people would be starving today when there is so much to share with them. We can start with one family at a time.

The Church's Mandate

I do know that Jesus did not feed or heal everyone he met or ministered to when he walked on earth. In fact, one can safely assume that for every one Lazarus he raised from death, there were many others who remained in the grave that day. For every five thousand people he fed, there were thousands more who went hungry. However, the Church has two clear mandates. One is to preach the gospel and lead the masses to the Lord as clearly indicated in Matthew 28:18-20. The Church is also mandated to feed the hungry as we find in James 1:27. It is not a matter of either/or but a matter of both/and. I know Christians can argue until the cows come home as to which one is more important or which comes first, just as long as we get the job done and not get stalled talking about it. We can take the time to debate on the methodology and not all that is bad. People need informed strategies to achieve lasting results. However, such endless arguments mean nothing to the over 1 billion poor who are hungry today. Such arguments mean nothing to the Milcah's and the Teca's of the world if they don't end up making a difference in their lives.

Stanley M. Mutunga

Chapter 7

Spirituality: A New Beginning

"John"

John is one of the most unassuming people I have ever met. Incredibly gifted academically, I first met him when he was in middle school. It was through his great-uncle that he was introduced to Tumaini. As a result of losing his parents, he almost dropped out in his junior year of high school. Like most kids in his situation would do, he began to look for menial jobs so that he could provide for himself and his sister. *"Although I was very young, the death of my parents left a very deep wound in my soul,"* John told me. He admits that the financial support from sponsorship has made it possible for him to continue with school, and now his future looks very bright.

It is, however, his spiritual conversion that he is most grateful about. While interviewing him in 2008, he said, *"...I gave my life to Christ and started the long journey to healing. In addition to the formal counseling, I must say though that it was the sharing with other children who had also lost parents that really made me realize that my situation was much better in comparison to other orphans and that I was not alone in the recovery journey."* He continued, *"Our collective determination to succeed gave me a renewed hope and my fears have been steadily decreasing. I actually look at the future now with a lot of hope and optimism than I did before attending my first camp."*

"Julius "

If there is one person who has undergone a 180% paradigm shift over the past few years, I would have to say it is Julius. Because of the stigma associated with HIV/AIDS, many orphans would not admit openly that the disease killed their parents. Not so with Julius. He has fully come to terms with the loss and has openly sought ways to heal and make something good come out of a bad situation. He vividly remembers how far he has come: *"When my parents died from AIDS, my sister and I were left without hope. Dad died in 1996 when I was only 8 years old and mom died six years later in 2002. After we buried mom, I told my young sister that we were done. We would never get anywhere."*

Like John, Julius is university material. He is set to start his college studies in early 2010. However, his biggest appreciation is not just the opportunity for education but a changed heart. *"The biggest thing that happened in my life when I first joined Tumaini was to accept Christ into my life. Knowing God through Jesus changed my world view completely."* To illustrate this change, Julius shared how he was initially planning to avenge the loss of his property to some unscrupulous relatives. *"Before I met Christ, I was ready to (exact) revenge on the relatives who had taken all my parents' property after they both died. I had to deal with a lot of bitterness—one taking care of my dying mom and watching helplessly as our property was being taken away. Tumaini took care of our basic needs,* *and although I haven't completed school yet, I am very optimistic. I can* *see hope on the way."* Watching Julius radiate God's love as he shares his new found love for personal enemies makes up for the challenges we face in Christian ministry.

"Rick"

I first met Rick some three years ago. An orphan and only in his mid-twenties, he was already leading one of the most successful ministries to AIDS orphans and widows in the Mathare slums. I sat down with him in the spring of 2009 to learn more about his background and love for the Lord. Rick's parents divorced when he was just 5 years old, and they later died when he was still very young. Growing up in Mathare slums, he used to complain a lot about everything. After the divorce and subsequent death of his parents, Rick became the sole guardian of his young sister. He remembers how she also got sick and died in his arms. He then became a homeless kid and did everything he could to survive on the streets. Rick hated God for allowing him to be brought to the world in such a dire situation and wondered why he couldn't have loving parents and go to school like other kids of his age.

One day, a "Good Samaritan" former neighbor picked him up from the streets and offered him a place to stay. Although the neighbor was a drug dealer, she helped raise him and even sent him to school. He told me how one day he was injured on his right hand and the doctor said it had to be amputated. On hearing the news about amputation, Rick got very scared and for the first time in his life, he went to church. He had heard through acquaintances that church people can pray for healing, and that is exactly what happened. He was prayed over and got the healing without having to undergo surgery!

It was through this miraculous healing that Rick began to think more about his life and his relationship with God. It wasn't long before he surrendered his life to Christ. As Rick recalls, *"After I gave my life to* *Christ, I felt an urge to begin figuring out how I could become part of the* *solution to the multitude of problems that the youths were facing in*

Mathare slums. I had been part of the problem, but I felt God calling me to become part of the solution."

In retrospect, it is his tough background that prepared Rick for the ministry that God was calling him to start. In 2005, Rick founded COMMUNITY TRANSFORMERS ("CT"), a Christian agency, with the sole aim of transforming the Mathare community, beginning with the youths and the HIV/AIDS patients. The organization is currently helping 250 youths, 98 of whom are HIV+. Some of the activities that CT does to attract area youth include drama, sports, music/concerts, modeling, talent shows, neighborhood clean-ups, and door-to-door visitations. Their biggest weekly event is a forum called *"Vijana Tusemesane" (which translates, "Youths, let's gather together and reason out")* taken from Isaiah1:18. The group meets on Saturdays to address the most challenging subjects facing the youth in the slums. This is a forum where all kinds of issues are addressed openly. Rick shared how in one meeting, a gun was turned in to the discussion leaders by a participant following a discussion on drugs and social ills that lead young people to commit murders in the slums. The discussions are that powerful.

Mike

Mike, a.k.a. "Mwau" ("the lost one") as he became popularly known in Kenya, has made one Vision Trip to Africa. He was there for less than two weeks. While in Kenya, Mike met and sponsored a little girl, and participated in the home visits delivering food and other supplies. However, his contribution was most deeply felt at the Christian camp as well as a local church. A relatively new believer himself, Mike gave a testimony that had an impact beyond anyone's expectations. In fact, the very first night he gave his testimony it instantly became the talk of town. Mike gave a moving talk of how God had delivered him from a life of drugs. It was not just that God had taken a drug addict and dealer and cleaned him up; it was also the confident way by which he told the story. Drugs had caused him to lose several family members and broken his marriage as well. During his testimony one night, he made a lasting impression on the audience by removing his denture to demonstrate how a lifetime of drugs had literally damaged all his teeth. Holding the denture from the little makeshift pulpit, he asked a pensive audience of nearly 400 teenagers, *"Would you like to be like me?"* You could hear a pin drop in the room at that moment. Many kids were moved to tears, and those who were already experimenting with drugs came forward for prayer and counseling. Little did he know that he had changed the course of life for nearly 50 kids present at that camp session.

During the next few days that Mike was in Kenya, he shared his testimony again at the camp and at a local church with amazing results. Mike may never go back to Kenya, but he left an indelible mark in the lives of many kids in just one week. There are kids who are free and clean today because Mike's testimony led them to quit experimenting with drugs, but also to submit their lives to Christ.

A Foundational Issue

One thing is certain in all of these stories: only God can bring about this kind of change. Only God can bring about this paradigm shift and begin a new thing in someone's life. The transformed lives of John, Julius and Rick illustrate a very important aspect of addressing the HIV/AIDS scourge in sub-Saharan Africa. Each of these young men represents not just a changed heart headed to heaven, but a changed worldview that has enabled them to look at life through new lenses.

At this writing, John is attending a prestigious university in Kenya and will soon graduate as an accountant. He is determined to reciprocate the grace that he has received through sponsorship by helping other orphans achieve their goals in life. Given his determination and resilience, there is no reason to think anything will stop him from realizing his goal.

Like John, Julius has a sharp mind mixed with incredible humility. He is an outstanding human being whose salvation experience brought about a total change in his life. His changed heart led to forgiveness of the extended family members that had taken advantage of his parents' death and usurped everything they had owned. He will be joining university in the spring of 2010 and like others, he is determined to not only succeed academically, but also be a channel of blessing to future needy children who have been otherwise forgotten by society.

In the case of Rick, he is simply an amazing young man. Humanly speaking, there is no reason he would be alive today given the life of extreme poverty and homelessness that he experienced growing up in Mathare slums. By all accounts, Mathare is one of the most unforgiving environments for a family to raise kids, let alone for a child to raise himself and his young sibling. How can one explain the resilience of a young boy who was taken in by a struggling drug addict and dealer and then grew up to complete high school (a huge feat in Kenya) and upon salvation change his heart so completely to have the presence of mind to gather his fellow thugs and lead them to a better option? And what about his choice to stay living in the slums so that he can help transform the community instead of moving out to safer zones? I will be the first one to admit that when I think of places to live in Nairobi, Mathare slums or any other slum in Africa for that matter does not come to mind as my first choice.

Rick's own conversion has brought change to thousands of other lives. He has not only founded a growing ministry but such key agencies as the Centers for Disease Control (CDC) have discovered him and trained him as one their HIV/AIDS counselors in the slums.

We may never know the real impact of Mike's testimony this side of heaven. What we do know is that decisions were made for Jesus as a result of Mike sharing his story. God used him to change the course of teenage lives, some of whom were headed straight for destruction.

A number of important themes emerge from the stories of these three incredible Kenyan orphans as well as Mike's testimony: the reality of sin; the need for intentional discipleship; the global nature of the gospel; and the process of a changed worldview.

The Reality of Sin

Friends, let's be real. By now we know that the optimistic promise by modernity that man will become better with more scientific knowledge has not borne fruit. If anything, with the technological advancement that we continue to witness every day, man has only become a better sinner over the past couple of centuries. Certainly, the post-modern era has only made man more confused and relativistic in the area of morality.

The one constant that has not changed is that humankind is still far too capable of evil by nature. The prophet Jeremiah put it well, *"The human heart is the most deceitful of all things, and desperately wicked..."* *Jer. 17:9 (NLT)* After the Fall of Man described in Genesis, all humankind is born with a propensity to sin. In fact, I believe that sin is at the core of the HIV/AIDS epidemic. Let me be clear, this is not to say that HIV/AIDS patients are worse sinners than you and me. No. What I am saying is that the existence of such an incurable disease that leaves millions of innocent children destitute is simply proof of sin's existence and the devastating results that it leaves on its trail. In reality, it does not matter who caught the disease first or how they got it. It does not matter whether the disease was contracted through unprotected heterosexual or homosexual activity, childbirth or blood transfusion. The cold, hard fact is, man is born a sinner and the consequences of sin are death—both physical and spiritual.

The reality is, innocent as the AIDS orphans may be, they like the rest of us are born as sinners. What happens to those who die before they can make decisions for Christ? An honest to this question for me is "I don't know!" However, based on the God of love that I see in the scriptures, I would be hard-pressed to believe that he would send them to eternal damnation. At least the story in *2 Samuel 12:21-23* of King David's reaction when he learnt of his child's death gives us a glimpse of hope for the children who die before they can make decisions for Christ.

In Romans 3: 23 (NLT) the Bible says, *"All have sinned and fallen short of the glory of God".* These AIDS orphans are not just economically forgotten but they are also spiritually lost. As a Christian working with AIDS orphans I see a fundamental importance of leading these kids to the Lord. This approach is critical to creating a future with hope because I believe that only Jesus makes a lasting difference in one's life. If we fail to intentionally bring Christ into the equation of helping orphans, they will remain forgotten even if their material needs are met.

My firm belief is that the best social programs will not reverse the tide of HIV/AIDS and other social challenges facing the youth of Africa. Clearly, hungry people will resort to anything to put food on the table, including some of the behaviors that are known to spread this killer disease. I am however convinced that faith in Jesus Christ and a strong biblical foundation is critical for reversing the fortunes of millions of forgotten AIDS orphans in Africa and beyond.

Call to Restored Lives in Christ

In order for social programs to have a lasting impact, Christ must be introduced. We must establish the fact that a restored relationship with God exists through Jesus. Christ must be front and center of all that we do in ministry. He is the bedrock in order for orphans to live fulfilling lives. Lasting positive change begins in one's heart and the order cannot be reversed. The Bible is very clear on man's standing before God. *"No one is righteous— not even one" Romans 3:10 (NLT)*. Paul goes on to announce both the consequences of unrepented sin and the blessings of a repentant soul: *"For the wages of sin is death, but the free gift of God is eternal life through Christ Jesus our Lord." Romans 6:23 (NLT)*

Books have been written on the subject of the so-called "age of accountability". The Bible is, however, silent on this subject. I believe that God works mysteriously in the hearts of people and that our responsibility is simply to share his word and trust that the Holy Spirit will convict sinners of their need to accept Christ. That is why for me it is a privilege to share Christ with orphaned kids at an early age, allowing them to live a full life in the hope of salvation. And for those who do accept Christ, we see it as our responsibility to nurture them in their faith and point them to Christ-honoring churches in their respective villages.

There is one passage of scripture that I have found profoundly relevant as I reflect on the spiritual development of orphans. The writer of Proverbs said, *"Direct your children onto the right path, and when they are older, they will not leave it." Proverbs 22:6 (NLT)* Although John, Julius and Rick do not belong to Tumaini and Community Transformers respectively in the context of a parent/child relationship, the two organizations are nevertheless the spiritual guardians and oases for these young men. In a very real sense whatever spiritual ideas are instilled in their lives today are critical for their long term formation as responsible adults in their respective societies.

The Glocal Nature of our Faith

One of my favorite topics with US Christians visiting Africa is to challenge the age-old mission approach. I say to them something along the lines that they do not bring God to Africa. God is already there. Rather, I remind them that God is bringing them to Africa to expose them to his doing so that they can find their niche and join him. I say this to dissuade the traditional approach that western Christians go to the developing world to 'teach them' about God. It really has allowed individual Vision Trip team members to open their eyes and see what God is doing in Kenya, also in them.

When teams visit during the TUBE, it has proven to be a wonderful opportunity for mutual learning and edification. This one week makes up for the loving and caring adult attention that most of these formerly forgotten children can only dream about. Many visiting donors are able to spend time with their child at camp and visit the family of their sponsored child. Visiting teams are provided a rare chance to get involved in the lives of the children in social, spiritual, emotional and economic levels all at once. Depending on the skills and spiritual gifts of the visitors, some are able to teach, others are able to do counseling and many more just play and make lasting friendships with these kids.

Worldview Change

An important aspect in salvation is exactly what changes when someone accepts Christ. What changed in the cases of John, Julius, Rick and Mike respectively when they invited Christ into their lives? Without getting bogged down into the anthropological details, I want to suggest that salvation ushers in a change of worldview, or a paradigm shift.

HIV/AIDS has reversed more than the little economic and health gains that sub-Saharan Africa had realized for nearly 50 years. The epidemic has also reversed cultural gains considered the norm since time immemorial. There was in place a reliable social security system built around the extended family with the strongest members of the family providing for the well-being of the elderly and the children. The fact that it is the bread winners who are being claimed by this disease makes AIDS the biggest threat to the families in sub-Saharan Africa. This is why I believe more than any other scourge that has affected Africa, AIDS is by far the worst enemy and it calls for a worldview change engineered by Christians.

Anthropology has taught us that cultures are dynamic and are always adapting and changing. Western and westernizing cultures change more rapidly in comparison to the more isolated and traditional cultures, but even those do change as well. As we have seen in the previous chapter, the children under study here have come to a world that has changed in some very dramatic ways: the loss of parents and grandparents in a dynamic time of modernity, urbanization and post modernity. The question is, how can we harness this change in a way that it turns out to be beneficial to the children and not harmful? When we talk of change, at what level are we talking about? Are we talking about merely surface or deep-level worldview change? If the latter, what is the role of the outsiders as well as the insiders in managing this change?

A fundamental aspect of addressing HIV/AIDS and other social ills affecting Africa is raising a generation that will think and act differently. I am fully aware that churches and Christian agencies do not make laws. The unjust laws or lack of laws that do not address the basic aspects of human rights, particularly as they affect women and children is a critical cause of the rampant sexual assaults on women. In much of Africa, male chauvinism is still upheld and this creates a situation where women and children have no say over their own bodies. Men freely do what they wish and in a context where the executive, the judicial and the legislature are not normally separated, justice for the weaker members of the society is still a distant dream.

The question for me then is, given the legal and political impotencies of non-governmental bodies, what can Christians do to tame the tide? I am convinced that we can do more than we realize. A few will need to get into those systems and change them from within, but the majority of us will have to bring about the change from the outside.

In his book published posthumously[72], Christian anthropologist Paul Hiebert says that when we introduce someone to the Lord, we must be cognizant of the fact that the gospel must penetrate three dimensions that are dominant in every culture. These three cultural dimensions are cognitive, affective and evaluative.[73] He explains them as follows: *"The Cognitive dimension...is the knowledge, ideas, beliefs, and worldviews...the conceptual content of a culture. That content provides people with linguistic categories with which to think, the logic they should use, and information about what exists and what does not. The Affective dimension...deals with feelings people have. And the emotions play an important part in all human relationships, in notions of etiquette and propriety, and in our ability to have fellowship... The Evaluative dimension ...values by which a culture judges human actions to be moral or immoral, proper or improper. Each culture also has its primary allegiances, its culturally defined goals, and its way of measuring success."*[74]

Many books abound on the subject of blunders that have been committed by well meaning cross-cultural missionaries. Many fail to appreciate the cultural differences and worldview complexities of their host cultures. No question the Holy Spirit does the convicting of sins, but following basic cultural clues in ministering internationally goes a long way.

I made my first major cultural blunder in my second month here in the US. It was in the 1980s and a church which had warmly welcomed me into their fold asked me to speak during a Sunday evening service. I jumped at the opportunity right away. During my two month stay, I had taken to heart what some of my American friends had told me while in Africa: "Americans don't like their old folks very much." I had heard something about "old people homes" and I could not understand why anyone would dump their loving parents into a home full of strangers when some of those same Christian friends lived in a mansion with one child, a dog and perhaps a cat, with plenty of room for an aging parent! So I gave it to them and told a hushed congregation that what they were doing to their old folks was wrong. I noticed after the service that some people were wearing long faces.

You see, I had come from a culture where old age was revered and the extended family took care of the older generation in a family setting. I was operating purely from an ego-centric position. In essence, I was drawing from my worldview—my cognitive, affective and evaluative up bringing—and imposing it on my American church friends. The fact is, even if I may have had a point—even a biblical point—my approach was culturally biased, and not well-received.

Ever since my late mentor and good friend Paul Hiebert introduced me to these three cultural dimensions over twenty years ago, I have become more intentional in recognizing the differences, albeit temporal, between people of different cultures.

It is important to ask the question: What changes when someone accepts Christ? When Julius, John and Rick became Christians, what really changed? Their hearts? Their minds? Their worldview? Everything? Did the gospel address all the three cultural dimensions—cognitive, affective and evaluative? What does Jesus mean when he said to the lawyer that he must love God with all his soul, heart and mind? Even more importantly, as people grow in the Lord and the need to address certain cultural practices arises, who should lead the charge for change- insiders or outsiders? Another Christian anthropologist, Charles Kraft[75], argues that the insiders must lead in addressing cultural behaviors that are counter to the Christian walk.

Here is my point. When people truly embrace Christ, he changes their deep-level cultural beliefs. This, however, is a process. Although all the three men discussed above have accepted Christ into their lives and they have started their journey, it is just that, a journey! They still have to confront their reality on the ground. They must wrestle with the corruption that is rampant in Africa. They must fully embrace Judeo-Christian principles and begin building a culture of respect for women and children, financial accountability and transparency, equality and uncompromised leadership, among other areas. While western brothers and sisters may come alongside and partner with their African counterparts to maturing as Christians, it is the African mentors, the role models, who understand the culture and who will effectively bring the best out of this young generation. This is not to say that outsiders cannot be effective cross-culturally, otherwise we would have no church today outside of North America and Europe. We must, however, work together in a complimentary manner, each playing their role.

Let me be very blunt: Unless the Church in Africa allows Jesus to change their thinking (cognitive), their feelings (affective) and their values (evaluative), we cannot successfully chase away the demons of greed, selfishness and corruption that have characterized the populace for so long. Maybe this is the generation that will change Africa. Rick's decision to become part of a solution to the problems facing nearly 800,000 slum dwellers gives me hope for the future. Julius' decision to forgive extended family members who took advantage of him and his little sister gives me hope for the future.

In a word, I am calling on the Church in Africa to begin building a culture that says "no" to the status quo and takes full responsibility for their own destinies, their churches, communities and, indeed, the entire continent. This is a long process but we are more than conquerors considering whose children we are.

Apostle Paul and Worldview Change

I believe that when Jesus said that *"I have come so that you may have life and life abundantly"*, he meant more than casual or superficial changes in believers' lives. True salvation does not mean instant glorification but it marks the beginning of a new journey. For most of us, it means a 180% turn.

Paul the Apostle's dramatic change of heart on his way to Damascus to persecute Christians (Acts 8) is not normative for every new believer, but it illustrates the effects of the gospel in one's life. Clearly for Paul, his thinking, feelings and values took a turn for the good and the transformation process began.

Paul's salvation led to a complete turn around and it affected not just him but also those who were around him and the church of Jesus Christ at large. True, Paul didn't suddenly become perfect, as he himself admits in several places in the New Testament. Romans chapter 6 and the Letter of First John chapter 1 clearly teach the need for Christian growth. Growth, however, is a process. The good news is that Christians are not alone, but the Holy Spirit is there to help in the transformation process. Paul was experiencing this gradual growth, or as some call it sanctification, in his

Christian walk and that is why he was able to counsel Christians in Rome on the same subject.

"And so, dear brothers and sisters, I plead with you to give your bodies to God because of all he has done for you. Let them be a living and holy sacrifice—the kind he will find acceptable. This is truly the way to worship him. Don't copy the behavior and customs of this world, but let God transform you into a new person by changing the way you think. Then you will learn to know God's will for you, which is good and pleasing and perfect." Romans 12:1, 2 *NLT*

It is significant that Paul's appeal to the Christians in Rome is not predicated on some social experience. Rather, he appeals to them to change *"because of all he [God] has done"* for them. People everywhere are deeply entrenched in their cultural worldviews at all the three levels identified earlier. That is why Paul's call for Christians to change their 'thinking' is critically important.

And So...

Back to where we began. It is tragic enough that millions of AIDS orphans and their families die forgotten, but that is not the only bad news. If we don't recognize the role of sin in the pandemic and intentionally mentor the likes of John, Julius and Rick to mature as men of God, we will have tragically missed the opportunity of a lifetime. No amount of social engineering will change hearts. Only God through Jesus Christ can bring about the kind of worldview change necessary to mend lives, rebuild communities, and end the needless suffering. The world doesn't need a committee of wise people to change it. Rather, it needs a few changed individuals whose lives have been turned upside down by Jesus and through sacrifice, grace and uncommon humility. Such men and women will lead Africa from its darkest hour of corruption, selfishness and untold greediness. During his visit to the country of Ghana in Africa in July 2009, US President Barack Obama singled out Ghana as a democratic example that other African nations must emulate. I applaud President Obama and appreciate his efforts in exposing the non-democratic countries and challenging them to change. However, democratization alone will not help heal all the wounds on the African continent, or on any continent.

John, Julius, Rick and Mike have begun a long journey. God is doing a great work of grace in their lives. I wonder what the Church can do to raise up more young men and women like these to change their communities, countries and even the world.

What is the Lord tugging your heart to do?

Stanley M. Mutunga

Chapter 8

Vision Trips: Life Changers

"Monique"

Monique lost her parents within a period of two years when she was in her early teens. With a rare level of leadership qualities, she assumed parental duties over her three young siblings. Although it has been quite a few years since her parents' demise, it is still evident that emotionally she still misses her mom. Monique is one of the few Tumaini children who have been visited by their donors in Kenya. Reminiscing on their recent visit, she told me how she treasured her experience with her sponsors. *"I have been blessed to have such a special relationship with my sponsors. Mike and Pat are not just donors to me, but I call them mom and dad."* I recalled when her sponsors were in Kenya a few years ago; watching Monique interact with Pat was especially poignant. She could often be seen firmly holding Pat's hand as if to say, *please don't leave me as my mom did.* Monique admits, *"It was a very moving experience for me and my siblings. All four of us are sponsored by the same (couple). Their coming to my home, the time we spent and the ensuing occasional correspondences has actually helped me to deal better with the past. Just the opportunity to call them mom and dad has been a blessing as I continue to heal from the emotional wounds of losing my parents. The experience has taught me that God is not limited to meeting my needs. He can provide other parents who are just as loving and caring. Because of my new parents, I will never be the same again."*

It has been interesting watching Monique transform from a young teen to a mature, 21- year-old woman now pursuing a career in pharmacy. She is filled with life and hope. There is no question that between being sponsored and eventually meeting Pat gave her the psychological satisfaction that she is not a total orphan anymore, but has a "mom" who lives in America. It definitely accounts for her growing emotional stability. Today, Mike and Pat talk fondly about "our children in Kenya" and the strong bond that has been formed between sponsor and child.

"Mike"

Mike is a typical hard working, middle class American family guy. A friend and dear brother in the Lord, I first met Mike some four years ago. He has led several Vision Trip teams from his church, and even his family of five has taken the trip to Kenya together. A family of modest means, they are always eager to share how they have been blessed by sponsoring four orphans. Mike is the kind of the guy who would drop everything to lead a Vision Trip to Kenya anytime he is called upon to do so. He explains why: *"My first Vision Trip to Kenya changed me completely. I saw orphans in their turf and how despite abject poverty, they seemed genuinely content. Their hospitality blew me away. The first trip also helped me to appreciate more what God has given me and my family and I wanted to give even more. I knew that was an experience I wanted my entire family to have and God enabled us to accomplish it. I know people have varying opinions about Vision Trips but for me there is no substitute to such trips if one wants to have a Christian global view of what is happening around the world."*

"Vickie"

Vickie first went to Kenya as a missionary with her late husband back in the late 1970's and ministered there until 1983. As a nurse, she served the community in that role until they went back to the US. In 1999, she went back to Kenya to speak on HIV/AIDS, especially its effect on women. During that trip, she spoke for three Sundays during which she discovered the lack of basic knowledge on the subject, especially on the accurate means of disease transmission. God brought to her mind the Bible passage that says, *"My people are destroyed for lack of knowledge." (Hosea 3:6a NKJV)* When they came back to the States, Vickie developed a big burden on her heart and began to earnestly pray, asking God to "please send someone" to work with the women she had met. She then felt that God said clearly to her, *you are the "someone" that I will send.*

For the next three years, she made numerous trips back to Kenya to work with the women who had so touched her heart. She started with nothing, staying in the homes of missionary friends and relying on public transportation. She was so driven to help these ladies and couldn't wait to make a difference, but success came much later.

Today, Vickie is the Founder and President of a growing Christian agency called Health Education for Africa Resource Teams (HEART) based in Nairobi, Kenya. They focus on health in general, however, one of their most successful programs is what they call WEEP—Women's Empowerment Equality Program. This program is aimed at rescuing and restoring one of the most vulnerable and forgotten populations, HIV+ widows with children living in the slums. HEART first helps with providing nutrition and medicines to keep these women alive and regain their health, then trains them in skills that regain their dignity and enable them to take care of their families.

Why Short-term Trips?

Perhaps the biggest umbrella question that many well meaning

Christians ask surrounds the legitimacy of short-term mission trips. This is a legitimate question because a lot of resources and time are invested in making these trips meaningful and successful. There are some who even question the legitimacy of western Christians seemingly invading other cultures and imposing their church cultures on the host communities. I will attempt to answer some of these good questions. Suffice here to say that if we embrace the idea of a global *wa kwetu* church, it addresses head on some of those legitimacy questions. As Christians, we belong to a family of God, a family of *wa kwetu* where we compliment each other according to the spiritual gifts that God has bestowed on each one of us. We must however confront some of the issues that come with short-term mission trips and make sure that they meet the intended purpose.

What are Vision Trips?

Vision Trips must be differentiated from the mere tourist sight-seeing safaris that many westerners take every year to Africa and other parts of the world. Vision Trips are not a form of extravagant voyeurism. Vision Trips are not opportunities for rich Christians to make a pilgrimage and "do something for the poor" to take away their guilt. Vision Trips are not even mission trips as we traditionally define them, where western Christians make trips to developing countries merely to do things for the poor.

Instead, as I see them, Vision Trips are opportunities for Christians to travel across the globe to learn… period! Vision Trips are wonderful forums for Christians to witness the needs of the host community, find out what God is already doing in that area and then join him in that good work. When we take Vision Trips, we are not "taking God" to the host community or country. The reality is that God is already there. Our role is to humbly discover him and join his cause. If we take this humble approach, then we can pray more intelligently and ask God, *now that I have seen what you are doing in this country/community, what is my niche? What would you have me or my church do in this part of the world?* We can pray as Vickie did, *please God, send someone*, and who knows- God just may end up sending us.

After leading some thirty Vision Trips over the last five years, I can confidently say that it is those "Visioneers" who take these trips with humility and open hearts and without pre-packaged answers for the poor who end up making a long lasting and positive impression on the lives of the host communities. The fact that Tumaini has focused on one country has had an impact on the area very significantly in physical and spiritual ways. The fact that Community Transformers has focused on Mathare slums has left a big economic and spiritual transformation in that part of the slum. The fact that HEART has focused the WEEP programs on the slums of Kibera and Mathare has made such an impact on the lives of the most vulnerable families. In each of these three Christian agencies, focused Vision Trips have enabled the agencies to reach more people in targeted communities and developed models that can be replicated in other similar contexts with modest adaptations.

Vision Trips Lead to a Glocal View

In a book entitled *Transformation: How Glocal Churches Transform Lives and the World,* Bob Roberts Jr., lead pastor at NorthWood Church in Keller, Texas, calls for Christian response to the global needs at two levels of transformation. He identifies these two levels as transformed life (T-Life) and transformed world (T-World). True transformation, he says, must start at a personal level. This then leads to the second transformation—that of the world. Regarding the first T, he recalls how he had to travel halfway across the world to find his own transformation. He then calls Christians to transformed lives. As he puts it, transformed lives will lead to proclamation of the word and a transformed world.[76]

Roberts' key point is that spiritual transformation is not an end unto itself. Rather, it is a basis for sharing that transformed life across the globe. Transformed lives will radically infiltrate culture and this new found world view will change not just the local context but global contexts as well. In other words, Christians don't just transform for themselves but it is a springboard for "glocal" missions. The mission itself is holistic in nature.

One can argue that, this is not really a new call. It goes back to the words of Jesus that the apostle Paul teaches in Acts 1:8, *"But you shall receive power when the Holy Spirit has come upon you; and you shall be witnesses to Me in Jerusalem, and in all Judea and Samaria, and to the end of the earth."* Yet what gives the call the urgency and freshness is the fact that over the last twenty years, Roberts himself has undergone a theological metamorphosis of sorts and successfully led his church and others to practice glocal Christianity. Already, his church has planted over eighty churches around the world.

What I find even more refreshing is Roberts' other book, *Glocalization: How Followers of Jesus Engage*. In this volume, he calls the transformed believers to take advantage of the fact that both the local and global contexts are getting better connected than ever before through technology, travel, business and communication. Following Thomas Friedman's *The World Is Flat*, Roberts says that the Church is in a better position than at any other time in her history to engage in glocal mission.

In the remainder of this chapter, I will marry some of Roberts' idea of glocalization and my experience with Vision Trips to craft a couple themes for the glocal 21st century church, including the place of Vision Trips in global mission; the impact that Vision Trips have made on real lives; and finally, the networking of churches and NGO's on the ground as a result of Vision Trips.

The Cases For and Against Short-Term Mission Trips

In Christian mission circles there have been legitimate concerns about the real gains for short-term mission trips, particularly trips to developing countries. A number of arguments have been advanced against the need for short-term mission trips.

One of the key arguments against short-term mission trips is the amount of money spent to fund the trips (including airline tickets, food and expensive hotels) could instead be used in doing more things for the poor. I had a missions pastor tell me one time that he will never go to Africa but will always give money to my ministry because he believes in what we do for the AIDS orphans. I told him that in the meantime we will gladly accept his money but will never give up trying to get him to Africa because of what I know such a trip can do to shape his mission paradigm for the future.

A second criticism has been that most team members on these trips appear to the locals more like rich tourists than missionaries. In his book,

When Charity Destroys Dignity, Glenn J. Schwartz gives an interesting illustration from a church bulletin advertising a mission trip to Mexico:

> *"[Our congregation] is sponsoring a women's only mission trip to beautiful Guadalajara, Mexico! We'll spend the week of June 11-18 in Guadalajara (also known as the shopping capital of Mexico!) where we will have the incredible opportunity to minister to, pray for, and teach women in a vibrant church community. And this trip isn't a 'rough-roach-in-your-bed' kind of experience either, we will be housed in nice clean hotel rooms, eat lots of salsa, and have plenty of time to shop! Our hope is to take at least fifteen women (including teenage daughters) on this Mexican Ministry Outreach...we trust that God will expand our hearts for Him as He expands our ministry to the women of Guadalajara. If you're remotely interested in this great commission adventure—or if you're just in the mood for Mexico after all this winter weather—call for more details about this fantastic outreach opportunity."* [77]

Well, if the focus is mere voyeurism more than outreach, it is not difficult to see why some would be skeptical about short mission trips.

A third criticism often cited is that not many souls are converted through these trips. Most reports back home focus more on the great pictures captured on the trips, the exotic foods and little or nothing about souls saved.

A fourth criticism is that teams do more harm than good to the host cultures. I found an interesting article on this topic that appeard in the Washington Post a couple of years ago. Acknowleding that mission trips across the board had become more popular, Neil says that mission trips *"...have come under increased scrutiny. A growing body of research questions the value of the trips abroad."* Acknowledging that these trips *"are supposed to bring hope and Christianity to the needy of the world,"* [78] the author goes on to add that critics of mission trips scornfully call them *"religious tourism"* undertaken by *"vacationaries."* Neil even gives some specific blunders made on mission trips. One example he gives was when a wall built on the children's soccer field at an orphanage in Brazil had to be torn down after the visitors left. In another case in Mexico, a church was painted six times during one summer by six different groups. And in Ecuador, a church was built but never used because the community said it was not needed. [79]

Some of the above arguments and illustrations may have been extreme, however, they do point to legitimate concerns that well-meaning Christians raise with respect to short-term mission trips. Some have argued that mission trips actually help the host cultures less than they do those who participate from non-poor countries. Based on my experience, however, I have found such trips to be extremely helpful to both the host culture as well as to the non-poor.

My perspective on short-term mission trips is completely different from those who do not see their value. In fact, I do not even like the phrase 'mission trips' because for me, it conjures an image of a western church going to do something for the poor in a developing country to make themselves feel better. Simply going to another country to do something for the people is not what I have in mind when I think of short-term mission trips, and this is why I prefer to call them *Vision Trips*. I need to mention just a few benefits for participation in Vision Trips.

Short-term Vision Trips are opportunities for the non-poor Christians to invest a little of what they have been entrusted so that they can attain what has been called a glocal perspective of the world. I know that with our ever-improving technology we can accomplish a great deal without ever traveling abroad. For example, we can now show very clear pictures or videos on HDTV and help someone sitting in their home in Maryland understand poverty in Malawi as much as possible without ever leaving their living room. Going on a Vision Trip to Malawi, however, will bring a completely different dimension on poverty than an HDTV ever could.

I believe that it is incredibly important for the non-poor Christians to have an opportunity to experience Africa, South America or South East Asia and not simply read about the various needs. I believe it is important to step outside of our comfort zones and experience a different kind of reality. It is important to breathe the air, smell the smells, ride on the bad roads in crowded buses, and worship in another language in the middle of nowhere, visit an orphan who lives with a 76-year-old grandmother in a thatched mud hut and embrace them even when you can't understand the language, because you still share the universal language of love and smiles. I think it is important to have your personal space invaded. It is important to experience a different concept of time where the event and the company are more important than the hours spent. I think it is important to travel and hang out with the likes of my late mom. Until her death in November 2009 at 92 years, I used to cherish my time with her whenever I was in Kenya. Mom didn't understand the concept of 'wasting time'. Her view of time was a never-ending cycle and she saw no problem with spending a whole day with guests just visiting because, as she put it, *"time is a cycle and God will bring back the same day again and again."* She used to wonder, *why the hurry.*

Vision Trip experiences connect the donors with their sponsored children in ways that cannot be achieved otherwise. Remember Monique, Pat and Mike? By their own admission, the lives of Monique and her sponsors Mike and Pat have been irreversibly changed because of a Vision Trip that was paid to Monique's home. These lifetime experiences connect the sponsors with beneficiary families and communities in ways that no correspondence ever will. In cases where orphans from multiple families are sponsored by one family or one church, Vision Trips by those families or churches connect these formerly forgotten AIDS orphans in ways that nothing else will. These kinds of experiences are priceless and they cannot be learned through any form of media, regardless of the flatness of our world.

Two Unforgettable Days

I have undertaken many Vision Trips and have experienced memorable occasions with various groups. I can vividly recall several situations during the home visits where God orchestrated events of mutual impact which will be etched in my mind for a long time.

Take for example the summer of 2005 when a team from a Southern California church was in Kenya. One day we visited a family and after talking and praying with the family one of the team members, Jack, stepped aside under the only tree on the small family compound and began to weep uncontrollably. The rest of us did not utter a word. We knew God had touched Jack somehow. He quietly proceeded to take off his shirt and left it to be used by one of the boys of the family. During the same trip, Ashley, a young lady on the team was moved by the love and commitment of one of the grandmothers we visited. She hugged, laughed and cried with the 70-year-old granny without saying a word in the local language. Before we left this particular home, Ashley noticed that the grandmother was walking barefooted in such a harsh environment and without a second thought gave her shoes away. For the rest of the day, Ashley walked barefoot under the scorching heat of the African sun. Although we all joked with her as she stepped gingerly the rest of the day long, this was a monumental event for her that she will never forget.

Or take another incredible day, summer 2009. It started out as a typical day of home visits. Well, there is nothing "typical" if you start the day by asking God to lead you and "do his thing" with you. We visited a home where three young boys lived by themselves. It was explained to us that the boys lived alone after losing their parents and their grandparents as well. Over the past few years, they had been under the care of an uncle who really loved them. However, he too had died in late 2008. The two older boys were sponsored and enrolled in a boarding school for most of the year, but the youngest- who was not sponsored- was left alone to fend for himself at just 12 years of age. Everyone on our team was truly touched by the situation. We could not understand why God had allowed such a young boy to be left alone. The idea of this sweet young boy fending for himself especially bothered Pastor Mike. Although he and his wife were already sponsoring another boy, before traveling back to the States, Mike offered to sponsor this 12-year-old too. As he explained it, the boy's predicament just could not go away from his heart and mind.

There was an interesting scenario leading to an incredible learning experience which took place during this same summer trip. One day, we went to the wrong home. *Oops!* What had happened is that we dropped in to visit at a home where we thought we had a sponsored boy. Sure, we found a boy and mother. The boy even had the exact same first and last names of the boy we were looking for. However, after interacting with the mother for a few minutes, I became suspicious that they were the wrong pair. It seemed like something was "off" but they wanted to answer all my questions 'right' so that we would give them the food we had brought with us. There were just enough inconsistencies in her story that led me to do a little investigative work. Sure enough, it turned out that she had tricked us into believing that she was the mother of a sponsored child who shared the same name with her son. I was more than a little bothered by the experience.

The following morning, however, we managed to find the correct home. It didn't take us long to realize that God really wanted us to swallow the disappointment of the previous day. As we interacted with the sponsored boy, his sickly mom and his grandmother, we discovered that there were three other unsponsored children in this family. Paul, the Kenyan Country Director for Tumaini, had not been with us the previous day and he began to sob as he learned more about this family's needs. You see there was this sickly boy in the family named Kevin who really touched Paul's heart, and God kept nudging him to offer sponsorship to the boy. Meanwhile, God was nudging my heart to sponsor a young 17-year-old sister named Lillian. At the same time Amy, another lady on the team, was sensing God's call to begin sponsoring the youngest girl of the family. Incredible! As we left that home, we all looked at each other and agreed that the devil himself had wanted to thwart God's work of changing the lives in this humble family by sending us to the wrong home the previous day. Despite the initial setback, we were still able to participate in awe of God's work.

For me, the important thing that happened in these few incidences was not so much *what we did*. What we did was an outcome of what God was already doing in our hearts. When God allows us to be touched by what we see through Vision Trips, the results are not just what we give but what God gives us—a completely different view of the his world, a glocal view if you will.

What is important is not that Jack gave up his shirt or that Ashley gave away her shoes. As heartfelt as they were, those things are temporary and will not necessarily change the lives of the recipients. Knowing the communal culture in that part of the world, it is fair to assume that the shirt became communal property for the boys in that village and it doesn't take too much imagination to see that it definitely did not last for long. The key is how well Jack connected with the level of poverty in that family and in that village. The shirt was simply symbolic of what was happening from the inside out. The same can be said about Ashley and her shoes. The 70-year-old grandmother had lived for 7 decades without ever wearing shoes, and by all accounts those shoes will not drastically improve the quality of her few remaining years. However, for Ashley, that was a defining moment and symbolic of the work of grace that God was doing in her life. For Pastor Mike, no amount of correspondence would have communicated the need of Nzuki, the 12-year-old boy needing sponsorship, as clearly as the home visit did. Standing outside their only house and imagining the lonely nights that this boy had been forced to endure spoke to him more than reading James 1:27 ever will. Seeing how Nzuki had been forgotten spoke volumes. To see Paul touched by the plight of young Kevin was a thing of beauty to watch—a non-poor Kenyan Christian doing his part to alleviate the situation of a poor fellow Kenyan Christian. Sometimes in ministry, we get used to the pain and suffering of our parishioners. It was refreshing to see that God is not just using Vision Trips to change the lives of western Christians, but also African Christians as well. Everyone involved came back as transformed individuals wanting to share their experiences and serve God in their specific niche of life. This could only happen during a Vision Trip.

Vision Trips Lead to Partnerships: A Few Case Studies

In the fall of 2003, I received an email from a former graduate student inquiring about the ministry of Tumaini. Jason had received a letter that I had sent to all graduate students early in the spring informing them of my decision to resign my Dean position at Hope International University in order to focus on building the fledgling ministry. In the spring of 2004, Jason invited me to Appleton, Wisconsin to meet and talk with him and his friends about a possible Vision Trip to Kenya. That summer, Jason and I led the first ever Vision Trip. Since then, Jason has led a summer Vision Trip every year to Kenya. Jason now serves as the Vice President for Tumaini and heads our mid-west regional base. About 100 Tumaini children are currently sponsored in the Appleton area.

I first met Roger in 2001. At the time I was the Dean of the School of Graduate Studies at Hope International University in Fullerton, California. Roger was the Lead Pastor at Parkcrest Christian Church in Long Beach, California. That particular morning Roger had invited me (as president and founder of Tumaini International Ministries) and a representative of another international Christian agency to a mission summit. After our respective formal presentations, we took time to exchange pleasantries during which time I shared with Roger my vision about Tumaini and what I deemed to be the critical role of Vision Trips. I talked to him about the millions of forgotten AIDS orphans in Africa and the need for the Church to respond.

In 2005, Roger and a team from his church joined me on their first Vision Trip to Kenya. As he puts it, even though this was not his first trip to Africa, it was completely transformational as it gave him an opportunity to meet real people with real needs. Since that first trip, Parkcrest has sent Vision Trip teams to Kenya at least once a year and a partnership has been formed with them in two critical areas: child sponsorship and the construction of a multi-purpose community center. Over 300 formerly forgotten orphans are now being sponsored through this partnership. As a church, Parkcrest has given tens of thousands of dollars for the construction of the Center. To honor their sacrificial giving, local Kenyans chose to name the main building in the Center as "Parkcrest Hall" in recognition of the gifts made by members of Parkcrest. I should note that the Parkcrest church did not request it, but Kenyan hospitality demanded it be so. In October 2008, a church was planted called Masii Christian Chapel where the locals are worshipping in Parkcrest Hall on a regular basis. Roger has since retired and the new Lead Pastor, Mike, is just as committed to this partnership and has already taken his first Vision Trip.

In early spring of 2005, Mike, Pastor of Cross Cultural Missions at Knott Avenue Christian Church (KACC) in Anaheim, California and I had lunch together where I told him about the mission of Tumaini. I then encouraged him to consider a Vision Trip to see for himself what God was doing and see if that was something his church may be interested in. Within weeks, a trip was arranged and Mike and I went to Kenya and spent twelve days seeing the hundreds of AIDS orphaned children who had been literally forgotten as people were busy burying their dead literally every day. On coming back, Mike knew that God wanted his church to partner with our small ministry to make a difference in the lives of as many children as possible. The result is that more than 350 children are now being sponsored by members of KACC.

In addition to child sponsorship and other special giving opportunities, the Women's Ministries at KACC have since partnered with us on a project that is dear to my heart. In 2008, Tumaini identified five widows who are HIV+ but after providing nutrition and antiretroviral drugs are stable and their health is improving. In partnership with the women, Tumaini has trained them as tailors and hired them to make school uniforms for over 600 Tumaini kids. The result is that these women who were on their dying beds are now healthy and have a reason to live. They not only have Jesus on their hearts, but are able to work and provide for their families.

In the summer of 2005, my wife and I joined the fellowship at Pathway Christian Church in Riverside, California. It didn't take long before the church leadership discovered our passion for working with AIDS orphans. Kerry, the senior pastor quickly caught the vision and planned for a Vision Trip in December 2005. On coming back from Africa, the church committed to sponsoring some 50 children. To date, over 100 kids are receiving sponsorship through the church and/or individual church members. Like other church partners, Pathway sends a Vision Trip team to Kenya every spring. In addition to child sponsorship, Pathway and Tumaini have partnered in identifying poor families that need livestock such as a cow or goat and matching them with the right animal.

In December 2005, Pastor Jim of Diamond Canyon Christian Church (DC3) invited me to speak at his church in Diamond Bar, California on World AIDS Day. I gave a summary overview of the devastation being caused by HIV/AIDS globally and Tumaini's role in trying to curb the effects. After the service, some of the orphans received sponsors. But more importantly, that talk led to a few church members expressing interest in a Vision Trip. In 2006, DC3 took a trip to Tanzania and Kenya, East Africa and some of the team members spent a day touring the area where Tumaini works and meeting their sponsored children. This partnership has continued to grow and a few more children are being sponsored by members of that church every year.

In 2006, I had a meeting with Mike, the Lead Pastor at Valley Christian Church in Chino, California and his colleague, Frank, the church's Missions Pastor. I shared with them the ministry of Tumaini and our emphasis on Vision Trips. In the following year, they made their first ever trip to Africa and a partnership was formed. The result has been nearly 100 children sponsored and a micro-finance project funded. In the village where the first micro-finance project was initiated, Mike is considered a co-pastor in the village local church. This past summer of 2009, the church sent a team of 16 members who joined the local staff in building a house for one of their sponsored children as well as participated during a TUBE Christian camp week.

In the summer of 2006, Cynthia from First Christian Church, Yuma, Arizona called me after listening to U2 lead singer Bono talk about the AIDS scourge. She had heard about Tumaini and wanted to see how she could get involved. I invited her to join a Vision Trip that December. We spent about two weeks in Kenya and she had a chance to see first hand the needs and pray about her future involvement. The result was that in early 2007, she led a Vision Trip of eight people from her church. Since then, nearly 300 orphan children have been sponsored by members of her church. During their second Vision Trip in the spring of 2008, they learned about the need to plant a church in the area and offered to partner with the local community. In October of the same year, the dream of a community church became a reality. Her church helped with some of the initial funding, but the local Kenyan community is now fully supporting the ministry.

One of the projects in the multi-purpose community center is a medical clinic that takes care of the needs of over 1000 AIDS orphans, their families and the surrounding community. Prior to the opening of our clinic, Knott Avenue Christian Church has been sending medical teams on Vision Trips to treat sponsored children. Some of the medical professionals on the KACC teams are connected to Joshua International Medical Group in Buena Park, California, and Tumaini is now forming a partnership with them. In a flat world context, we are exploring ways for the two medical centers to work together seamlessly—though one is

Masii, SE Kenya and the other in Southern California. Once all of the necessary permits and paperwork is in place, we envision enabling a nurse in Kenya who can work closely with doctors in Buena Park on a daily basis in referral cases.

I believe Vision Trips have played a critical role in opening the eyes of so many who had otherwise never traveled outside of their comfort zones to see how the rest of the world lives, and now can see how best to invest in other people's lives—one orphan at a time. Vision Trips have clearly been pivotal in getting churches involved. The result has been that thousands of children and their families have been transformed in both physical and spiritual areas of their lives. I see the all of the above stories as just the beginning of the work that God has allowed us to be part of at Tumaini.

Jesus' Ultimate Example of Identification

Every time I lead a team of American Christians to Africa on a Vision Trip, I give the same speech somewhere mid-way through the trip. At this point, the honeymoon begins to give way after missing some of the conveniences they are used to enjoying back home. I thank the team for coming and remind them that in this part of the world, there is nothing "exciting" to see. SE Kenya is not a tourist attraction by any stretch of imagination. There is absolutely nothing to see but people. Such moments lead me to think about the following scriptural passage. Writing to the church at Philippi, Apostle Paul wrote the following: *"You must have the same attitude that Christ Jesus had. Though he was God, he did not think of equality with God as something to cling to. Instead, he gave up his divine privileges; he took the humble position of a slave and was born as a human being. When he appeared in human form, he humbled himself in obedience to God and died a criminal's death on a cross."Phil 2:5-8 (NLT)* I see Jesus' coming to dwell among us as the ultimate model of identification so that he could fully understand the condition of our human frailty and eventually die on the cross for humanity. I wonder how it must have felt for Jesus to be the only God on earth. Was it lonely down here sometimes? Did he miss being home in heaven? Did he miss the use of ultimate power every now and then? How must it have felt not to have a permanent place he could call home?

There is no way we can equate a two week Vision Trip experience with Jesus' coming to earth, especially when we consider the ultimate price that he paid on the cross. On the other hand, I see the parallel in the sense that Vision Trips are the closest thing for non-poor Christians to have a glimpse of what the majority of the world's poor go through on a daily basis. Vision Trips are not opportunities just to sympathize with the conditions of the forgotten AIDS orphans and widows but instead to truly connect in the most authentic way and learn from people who have lost so much yet are some of the happiest and most generous people on earth. Our giving them some material help then becomes an act of worship.

Vision Trips are Transformative Experiences

I agree with Bryant Myer's point that the end result of international Christian development should be changed lives—that of the non-poor (donor), the Christian agency staff and the poor[80]. Vision Trips are designed to be transformative. In mission circles, the prevailing idea seems to be that we go out there to "convert them" or "sink wells for them". In other words, we tend to think that missions as just about the poor. If that is all we accomplish, then we miss the more important point in the whole endeavor. Jesus came so that we might all be changed—the poor and non-poor, the believer and non-believer alike.

Yes, Vision Trips do lead to child sponsorship. God uses the exposure to connect the non-poor with otherwise forgotten AIDS orphans. Many times, those orphans end up accepting Christ and of course, they receive basic material help to alleviate their poverty situation. But what about the sponsor, the non-poor? These need to be transformed just as well. The exposure alone on such a trip leads the sponsor to appreciate how much we have here in the western world. For true transformation there needs to be something much deeper than a mere emotional response that is short-lived. It must lead to the long-term strategic change that affects our view of stewardship of the material wealth that God has entrusted to us.

For those of us serving on a Christian agency staff such as Tumaini, it is a humbling experience to realize the awesome responsibility and opportunity we have to connect the needs of the millions of forgotten orphans with the non-poor who are willing and open to be used of God.

We stand between the sponsor and the needy and we have the highest call to get it right. We should never reach a point where we get used to the job. We need the Lord to keep us fresh and pray as Bob Pierce prayed years ago, *"let our hearts be touched by the things that touch the heart of God."*

Chapter 9

Micro-Finance Partnerships: From Deathbed to Seamstress

"Susan"

Susan is a 38-year-old widow and lives in the rural area of Machakos, Kenya. When I first met her in the summer of 2005, she was very weak due to her HIV+ status. Her husband had died a couple of years earlier from AIDS and it seemed it was a question of time before she would succumb to the same disease. At that time, one of her sons was sponsored, but two more were on a waiting list for sponsorship. Before we left her home, she took me aside and expressed concern that she was running out of time and it seemed to her that I had forgotten her other two children. I assured her that I had not forgotten her two other children but more importantly, God had not. My words calmed her for a few minutes but it was clear that given her health condition, she was worried about what would happen to her children should she die before they could get any help. Looking in her eyes, she had lost hope and succumbed to the fact that her children would join the ranks of other forgotten orphans.

Little did Susan and I know that while we were busy talking, someone on the visiting team had fallen in love with her oldest son and had offered to be his sponsor. In the months that followed, the other remaining child was also offered sponsorship.

As I normally do in such situations, I gave Susan a small talk. *"Look, you are the only mother to these children. You are the only one best suited to take care of them. To do that, however, you need to admit your health situation. Get tested for HIV so that they can determine the right medication for you."* At the time, the government plan of free ARV's (antiretroviral medication) was not yet in place, but through child sponsorship, Tumaini was able to help the surviving parent in some small ways such as this. Although Susan seemed to listen actively to what I said, I could tell due to the stigma associated with HIV, she was nervous and reluctant to get tested. I was overjoyed when I learned that Susan had voluntarily agreed to follow my advice and go for testing.

A year later, I took another team to Susan's village. She realized that I didn't recognize who she was so she came and introduced herself to us. It was obvious that the medication had worked and she had gained some healthy weight. Even better, you could see life and hope in her eyes again. Truly, God had done a miracle in her body and she was ready to live and take care of her three children.

In 2007, Tumaini initiated micro-finance projects to help address poverty in a more comprehensive manner through a program dubbed People Overcoming Poverty (POP). Under this program, a pilot group of five women was formed, all HIV+, and they were enrolled in a tailoring program teaching them how to become seamstresses. As I write this book, the training is complete and they have been hired back by Tumaini so that they can make school uniforms for hundreds of Tumaini sponsored kids who are in elementary schools across the region. Talking with Susan about the program, she compared it to *"throwing a lifeline to those who are sick and literally giving them an opportunity to not just survive but actually live quality lives and make a contribution to their own families and society again."*

"Nora"

Shifting gears, we move some 92 kilometers or 58 miles NE to Nairobi, to the Mathare slums and meet Nora. A 38-year-old mother of three, Nora was introduced to HEART in a similar (if not worse) situation as Susan. She narrated to me how she was sick in bed and waiting to die. Having been diagnosed with HIV a few years back, there was nothing but poverty in the slums and she had no chance of surviving much longer. Like other mothers, her biggest concern was her three little children she was about to leave behind as orphans in a matter of a year. She knew that upon death, the orphans would simply be forgotten.

A Christian neighbor of Nora's had heard about HEART and their ministry among HIV positive mothers. Given her deteriorating condition, Nora didn't think an intervention at this stage would do her any good. She initially declined the offer. Nevertheless, the neighbor was persistent and the HEART staff was able to meet Nora at her little shack in the slum.

Through HEART, Nora was given an opportunity to access ARV's and within a couple of months, she was literally able to wake from the doors of death back to life. She then enrolled in one of their WEEP programs in the slum. WEEP identifies mothers who have been widowed or abandoned when their husbands learned of their HIV status. WEEP commits to providing medical care, nutrition, vitamins, rent assistance and access to ARV drugs. HEART also assures that the children have school uniforms and necessary resources to attend school. In a word, WEEP equals keeping mom alive, healthy, and employed and their vulnerable children from becoming orphaned[81].

"Christie"

Christie is a 32-year-old HIV+ woman. A widow raising a 12-year-old son, Christie lives in Mathare slums. Like Susan and Nora, she was in very similar circumstances. She was on her deathbed when she was literally discovered by Community Transformers. After being diagnosed with the deadly disease, there was very little hope for Christie. She remained a worried woman as she thought about the future of her son growing up without parents and no hope. She knew that he would likely join the thousands of forgotten orphans roaming in the slum of Mathare and his fate would be dictated by the social ills in that unforgiving environment.

It was during this darkest of hours that the staff of Community Transformers learned of Christie's dire situation and came knocking her door. They helped her access antiretroviral drugs and basic food supplies. With counseling and networking with other agencies that could help, Christie found her old self again. One of the hallmarks of Community Transformers is assistance with small business start-ups. Their model is to give small loans initially, and if the recipients have been successful with their start-up, then they receive bigger loans as needed. It turned out that prior to her illness Christie had been a successful seamstress and was running her own small business. When she became sick, however, all the funds were depleted. So it was good news when Community Transformers offered to help her with funding to re-start her clothing business.

The morning I visited Christie at her shop in the spring of 2009, she was a very happy woman, telling me that she had found her live back again, and she is able to support herself and her young son. What is more is that Christie has found faith in Jesus. Although she remains HIV+, the right use of ARV drugs and proper nutrition had given her energy back. She was excited to tell me that she had a contract to make school uniforms for 34 neighborhood children in the slum, a small success by most standards, but one able to support her in the surrounding economy. Most importantly, I was gratified to learn that Christie is now training other HIV+ women in the same skill so that they too can be self-reliant.

Lame for 38 Years!

When I think of the conditions of millions of forgotten orphans and widows, one story in the Gospels that registers vividly is the encounter between Jesus and the lame man recorded here in John chapter 5:

"Crowds of sick folks—lame, blind, or with paralyzed limbs—lay on the platform (waiting for a certain movement of the water, for an angel of the Lord came from time to time and disturbed the water, and the first person to step down into it afterwards was healed). One of the men laying there had been sick for thirty-eighty years. When Jesus saw him and knew how long he had been ill, he asked him, 'Would you like to get well?' 'I can't,' the sick man said, 'for I have no one to help me into the pool at the movement of the water. While I am trying to get there, someone else always gets in ahead of me.' Jesus told him, 'Stand up, roll up your sleeping mat and go on home.' Instantly the man was healed! He rolled up the mat and began walking." (LBT)

As the story unfolds, we learn a little bit about the lame man. Most importantly, he had laid by the pool of Bethesda in infirmity for 38 years! At first glance of the text, it sounds interesting that Jesus would even ask the question, *would you like to get well?'* Surely, Jesus being God and knowing the situation of this poor guy could have simply offered the healing. I mean, why did he need to ask the question? For goodness sake, the only reason the poor man had laid by the pool and waited there for 38 years was that he wanted to get well. A closer look would suggest that it was a very legitimate question. You see, people are not robots. God created us with a free will so that we can think and decide as to whether or not we want change in our lives. What I find puzzling is actually the man's response to the question. When asked a direct question, rather than saying, *'yes sir I want to get well'*, he gave a rather pessimistic response, "*I can't for I have no one to put me into the pool.*" (Emphasis added)

It seems clear from the passage that Jesus deliberately chose one of the most dramatically helpless sufferers in the crowd in order to display the limitless power and grace of God. It is important to note that he deliberately healed the lame man on a Sabbath day even though he knew it was considered against the law. (Lev. 23:3) By doing a good act on this day, Jesus wanted to expose the heartless hypocrisy of the Jewish leaders.

By all accounts, the lame man remained passive during the healing experience. By his own admission, he was at the bottom of the pile in terms of the disadvantaged folks in his town. His infirmity was so severe that he couldn't move fast enough. He had been by-passed by others faster than him for 38 years.

If we fast-forward this incident two thousand years, this becomes an all-important lesson for us today. Today we live with the disadvantaged who are in very similar conditions. The one billion poor still respond in the same way: *"I can't."* For the people who need and deserve help, some have given up hope because they have *'no one to put them in the pool.'* They have been forgotten for way too long. They have resigned themselves to a life that is less than what God intended. Just as Jesus exemplified in this story, it will take Christians to proactively stretch out a hand and offer the assistance needed. You see, it took intentional partnerships to connect Susan, Nora and the Christie to the "healing pool". By God's grace, these three women have been offered a second chance for life.

Snapshot of Three Partnerships

It takes not only *searchers* to bring hope but also teamwork. I have seen a semblance of that partnership in the three Christian agencies of Tumaini, HEART, and Community Transformers. Let's take a closer look at the programs and partnerships that were instrumental in assisting Susan, Nora and Christie and many others in similar situations.

1)   People Overcoming Poverty

People Overcoming Poverty (POP) is a division within Tumaini that is geared towards selectively helping the HIV+ widows and the poor in general within the Machakos region with a hand-up. As previously mentioned, it was in the fall of 2007 when Tumaini first partnered with the Women's Ministry at Knott Avenue Christian Church to support a pilot project in Kenya. Tumaini identified five HIV+ widows who we knew were sick and stigmatized in the community. We felt it was important to seek out the most needy and attempt to make a difference in their lives. In the initial stages, it was important to ensure that they had anti-retroviral drugs to get them healthy before they could undertake a major physical project. They expressed interest in learning how to make clothes, so Tumaini then shared the idea with the Women's Ministry at KACC and $5,000 was raised to fund the project. The funds were used to hire a teacher, rent a space, and buy the necessary materials for the training. Because the women were physically weak and four of them had to walk an average of six miles one way three days a week to come for classes, training that would normally take about seven months took a year for them to become proficient. In the fall of 2009, Tumaini hired the women to make school uniforms for more than 600 Tumaini children. We hope to attract business from the community and if need be, open more tailoring shops.

POP has given these formerly forgotten women several things, the most immediate being that they now have a reason to live. They have found hope and now look forward to making a living for themselves and their families. They don't have to rely on charity but have regained their dignity and will now become contributing members of the society. The fact that Christians have given them this new hope will likely influence their decisions for Christ in the months to come.

2)   WEEP
HEART'S vision is to empower the people of Africa to survive the HIV/AIDS pandemic. Women's Empowerment Equality Project (WEEP) is a division of Health Education Africa Resource Teams (HEART). HEART does its work mostly in the slums of Kibera and Mathare in the city of Nairobi, as well as in other rural parts of the country. The goal is to help women who are HIV+ and raising their families alone because their husbands either are dead or have deserted them. The rationale is that it is better to help these women and keep them alive as long as possible because they are the ones best suited to raise their own children. Once physically stable, mothers are taught a trade and provided a job at a WEEP center. In a country where the unemployment rate is estimated to be between 40% and 60%, a job allows the WEEP women to provide for their families in a way that would be impossible without this project. Beyond the devastatingly high unemployment level, the lack of information and the stigma associated with AIDS make it nearly impossible for an HIV+ woman to secure employment, support their

children, or access ARV drugs. WEEP's objective is to provide training so that HIV+ women may break the cycle of ignorance and poverty so many are caught in. The first WEEP program was started in 2005 with five women who were HIV+. These women were simple charcoal dealers and mosquito net tailors.

One common thing about all the five original WEEP women is that before they were trained in a skill, they totally depended on HEART for all their basic supplies. After their training, they now are able to meet most of their basic needs. Getting their health back has been instrumental.

What I find providential is the way HEART got funding for this project. According to HEART President, Vickie Winkler, when they were developing a vision for this ministry, God was speaking to someone they had never met in Massachusetts. Dr. Peter Norris Rogel (Founder of Norris Rogel Foundation) was doing a Google search for an organization to fund when he found HEART. He liked their WEEP program and what it was intending to accomplish and decided to fund it. Since then, the foundation has been sending $5,000 to HEART every month to make 500 mosquito bed nets. A program that started merely four years ago with five women is now serving 53 women and over 300 kids.

3)   Community Transformers

The founders of this ministry are young men and women who were born and raised in Mathare slums. Being orphans themselves, the founders fully understand the socio-economic challenges that people in the slums undergo on daily basis. Their decision to stay in the slums even when they had opportunities to move out to safer parts of town is what has drawn many donors (mostly local) to this amazing group. They start by providing small loans for start-up businesses and graduate to larger ones as people, mostly HIV+ widows, repay their loans. As we saw in Christie's case, they have completely transformed quite a few lives in the slum.

Founded in 2005, the ministry's sole aim was to transform the Mathare community, beginning with the youth and the HIV/AIDS patients. CT is currently helping 250 youths, 98 of them are HIV+. Their biggest event is *"Vijana Tusemesane."*[82]

The Power of Partnerships

Christians have in their power the ability to touch and transform the lives of millions of deserving but forgotten HIV+ widows and their families. It doesn't take a lot of money to make a tangible difference in the lives of the poor in the developing world. However, it does take an intentional, glocal view.

As I reflect on the spiritual and physical transformation that Susan, Nora and Christie have each undergone the one common denominator in all three cases is partnership. In Susan's case, there is the partnership between Tumaini and the Women's Ministry at Knott Avenue Christian Church in California. In Nora's case, there is a partnership between HEART and the Rogle Foundation in Massachusetts. In Christie's case, there is a partnership between Community Transformers and local Kenyan donors.

Not the Amount that Counts

It is not the amount of money donated that counts. We do not need millions of dollars to make a difference in the lives of the forgotten—the orphans and widows. It takes just a few Christians willing to take God at his word, share their vision with the church of Jesus Christ and leave the results to God. I know that for some individuals or churches, a one-time gift of $5,000 sounds like a lot of money, and for some, it is. However, the amount itself pales in comparison to what it can do in the lives of five unemployed, sick widows who are trying to provide for their families. It can give them back their health. It can provide a trade skill for them to earn a living. As they become contributing members of society, it can give them back some of the dignity that was taken away by their HIV status. Most importantly, it can provide opportunities for them to learn about the eternal life that Jesus offers. For those who cannot afford $5,000, there are other options as we have learned from Community Transformers organization. In a country where the average person lives on less than $2.00 a day, small, incremental amounts can help the poorest of the poor to provide for their families.

Not About Us

One of the biggest temptations in Christian development is the need for the donor to want to control what happens on the field. I am not talking about accountability because, no matter who we are, we need to be accountable first to God but also to trusted friends in ministry. I am talking about paternalistic behavior. This is natural because we feel that since we have invested money, we must also control every aspect of how it is spent even though we do not know the nuances of the local needs and how best to meet them. Somehow, we have a limited or selective application of what partnership is or should be. I personally struggle with this balance every single day. I want to give but also want to tell them how to use my every penny. It should not be so if we have a system of checks and balances in place. Helping the poor is really not about us, it is about them. We know they are poor but many a times we also think we know the solution to all their problems. The truth is we don't. Let me introduce you to a concept that has really helped me as I work with the poor.

Assets Based Community Development (ABCD)

I have always liked the Assets Based Community Development (ABCD)[83] approach to helping the poor. This model allows us to go into a community with an open heart to see things through their own eyes rather than coming with pre-packaged answers. Through this approach, we simply ask the question, *'what works here and how can we come alongside and work with you as you address your socio-economic needs?'* I especially find the five steps of the ABCD approach helpful and, in a nutshell, these are the basic community development steps that I think Christian agencies will find most useful. Of course, I tell them that I only do what I do out of my love for Jesus and that I will never leave him out of the equation. Africans being such religious people, I have not met any resistance to the gospel. I am still learning.

> *Step1: Mapping capacities of the people in communities*
> *Step 2: Building relationships within communities*
> *Step 3: Mobilizing communities for economic development*
> *Step 4: Developing a vision and plan*
> *Step 5: Leveraging outside resources to assist communities* [84]

Those of us who have served the poor in the developing world for some time know that these steps are critically important if followed to the letter. They surely save us a lot of headache. However, in practice, what I have seen on the field is that because most of us non-poor operate from a microwave mind-set, i.e., we want to see the results **now**. Many times we want to start with step five and throw money to the poor, though we may have little or no understanding as to the local priorities and complex cultural issues.

I remember a conversation I had several years ago with a Christian agency leader from Ghana. She told me of an international Christian organization that went to Ghana and offered to address the issue of guinea worms. Evidently, guinea worms were killing many villagers and the organization came up with what they thought was a perfect solution: providing clean drinking water. They then urged the locals to support the sinking of wells for clean water and told them not to consume the stagnant water anymore, as it was the cause of guinea worms. Scientifically, that was the right solution. The only problem is that the locals did not see it that way. In their worldview, they did not see any connection between dirty water and guinea worms. As far as they could remember, the community had always relied on the water and they saw no need to change their lifestyle. Someone did not take the necessary time to understand the situation from the locals' perspective. Someone did not begin with addressing the community where they were and move with them to the unknown. All the first four steps were skipped and so it's no wonder a well-meaning Christian act turned into a controversial project.

Helping the poor is a partnership between the non-poor, the staff of the agency and the poor themselves. Each of these parties is an incredibly important stakeholder. Even in the case cited from John 5, Jesus asked the question, *"Would you like to get well?"* Even though as God, Jesus knew everything about the lame man, he did not presume to know that the man actually wanted to be healed from his infirmity. Even though by virtue of being by the pool there was every indication that he wanted to be healed, still Jesus did not presume that was, in fact the case. So it is with community development.

There is dignity when we go in humility to the poor who live in the villages and slums of Africa, SE Asia and parts of South American cities and humbly ask, *how can we come alongside to give you a hand-up?* If the right questions are asked first, funding is usually not a problem and we end up funding the projects that the communities need the most help with. I am continually learning how to work better with the poor. In my short period as the president of a growing Christian agency in Africa, the poor have taught me that the two areas where they need my partnership the most are *healthcare and education.* Whenever I have been humble enough to ask, they have told me that if they have good health and their children get a good education, other needs will be met, some in a short time, others will take more time but eventually will be addressed. The more I have thought about it, the more I think they are right. Widows need to be healthy and they will toil to no end for their children. Kids need good health and quality education. Education will be a ticket to addressing all other socio-economic issues for them and their countries.

Let me introduce you to yet another helpful concept.

Appreciative Inquiry (AI)

Appreciative Inquiry is a postmodern approach that encourages us to move away from the traditional rationalistic and mechanistic approach to research, including research that pertains to understanding poor communities. In its simplest form, it is a call to begin looking at life from the perspective of the community we are attempting to help. The assumption is that since the community already exists, there must be certain norms that have held it together for generations, way before we showed up. It sounds like a common sense approach but it is not what most of us assume when we move into a traditional community. A case in point is the guinea worms scenario in Ghana that I cited previously. What the well-meaning Christian agency forgot to consider is that even though guinea worms were killing people, the locals had never connected water to death. How can water that had sustained them since time immemorial also be the cause for death? It sounds like a no brainer to those who of us who operate from a modern and mechanistic worldview, but not so to those who don't share our perspective. Like the ABCD model, proponents of AI call development agencies to focus on finding out what works in a community and build on that rather than re-inventing the wheel.

Building on the earlier works of David Cooperrider and Suresh Srivastiva[85] and Johnson and Ludema[86], Bryant Myers calls Christian development agencies to consider these questions when we go into partnerships with the poor of the developing world: *"What allows the community to function at its best? What possibilities await the community that will allow it to reach for higher levels of heath, vitality and well-being?"*[87]

I have found the diagram below helpful as I conceptualize my work in a poor community. The first step is <u>discovery</u> of what gives life. Such a discovery will lead the Christian agency staff to <u>dream</u> of what might be. This is the vision stage followed by a <u>dialogue</u> which I insist must be respectful. The final state is then <u>delivery,</u> which must be sustainable for the long-term.

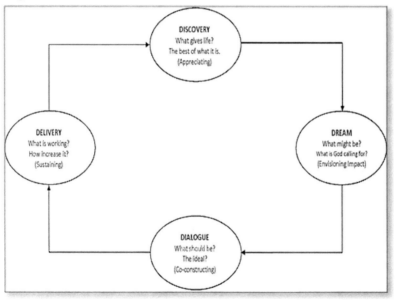

Source: Visioning through Appreciative Inquiry.[88]

It is a humbling experience to go to someone that you can see is dying and ask him or her the question, *how can I come alongside to help you?* I don't know about you but I find it easier to just go and figure it out for them and provide the solution. Unfortunately, history is not on our side on this one. Quick fixes, especially when they don't involve the poor, are never long lasting.

I consider it a privilege to have met Susan, Nora and Christie. I don't know how long these women will live but that is beside the point. By God's grace, they have been helped into the 'healing pool' and they are no longer lame. Someone proactively went to his or her turf as Jesus did with the lame man. Someone asked the question, *do you want to be healed,* and they answered in the affirmative. When we come down to it, the real connectors here were the neighbors who pointed Susan to Tumaini, Nora to HEART and Christie to Community Transformers.

One Final Call

Unfortunately, for every Susan, Nora and Christie, there are millions of others waiting by the poolside. Some like the lame man, for 38 years- no kidding! If HIV/AIDS is the greatest humanitarian challenge of the 21st century, then it is urgent and critical for the Church to ask the question, *how can we come alongside and be of help.* The Church, the people of God cannot afford to maintain a deafening silence when a billion poor people are waiting for someone to help them to the healing pool. Can we afford to?

Chapter 10

Healthcare:
When Little Means Much

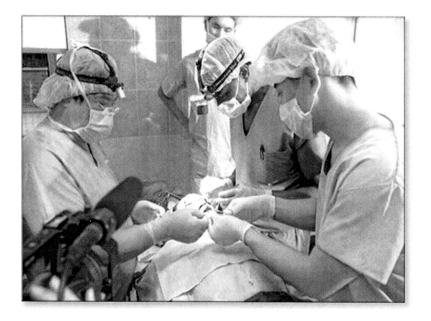

"Ron"

"Quite honestly, I have been doing Medical/ Dental relief missions for the last 19 years now. The trips have numbered over 20 and I have found myself in at least 10 different countries on four different continents. Never in my life would I have pictured myself doing such trips when I graduated from my residency 28 years ago! In retrospect, though, I can honestly say that I never really knew why I became a dentist

until I started doing these relief missions! I'm sure the lifestyle was appealing at first, but with time, the financial rewards dwindle and leave you somewhat empty, in search of more rewarding gratification.

After finding myself in these remote villages, I found that relief (in the form of tooth extractions, tumor removal, wound suturing, and infant deliveries) could be provided on site and without the need of a hospital! ...Dentistry, by its very nature, is a science and practice that doesn't require electricity and can be performed in the most remote areas. It provides immediate relief to the people...

For those who adopt a Christian theology, we are asked to use our God-given gifts to step up and use these gifts given to us as God wills. He has a gentle, but definitive way of reinforcing these actions on His behalf... for me personally, it was satisfying that deep, longing to feel that I was making a difference for the good of my fellow man. We are commanded to provide relief because this is God's nature. As always, he says what he means and means what he says! In return, he reshaped my priorities... for my own peace of mind! Today, instead of looking forward to the new Mercedes or the two week vacation sitting on a beach someplace with an "umbrella drink" I now look forward to going into "unreached" areas and providing immediate relief from pain. The satisfaction and rewards are overwhelming... and are truly far greater than I could have ever imagined from the expectations I had when entering dentistry initially." [89] *~Dr. Ron Jurgensen*

"Lonny"

"During our 16 day service in Kenya we were blessed to be able to see about 500 local villagers from the Machakos and Masii region of Kenya. This region is about 2 ½ hours southeast of the capital city of Nairobi. This region of Kenya has been stricken not only with HIV/AIDS,

but also with a drought. During our initial 4-day clinic to the community, our Medical and Dental team were able to do the following:

- *Treated over 500 local villagers*
- *Pulled several hundred teeth*
- *Saved over a hundred teeth via either filling cavities or performing Root Canals*
- *Diagnose and dispense hundreds of needed Rx for various illnesses*
- *Screened 15 patients for surgical procedures in Nairobi*
- *Shared God's love and grace through Jesus Christ in song, skits and witness*

Due to the rural conditions, electricity was intermittent; so much of this work was done via flashlights. Our ability to provide for these 500 patients was truly a gift from God and was not part of our original plan.

The following 2 days we were able to see about 200 Tumaini children during the beginning of a weeklong VBS program. We distributed deworming medicine and vitamins and screened and treated the children for a variety of conditions.[90] ~Lonny Myers, Executive Director of Joshua International Medical Group

"Joyce"

Joyce was one of the lucky patients who managed to see "Dr. Ron" when he made a Vision Trip to Kenya in the spring of 2009. I say lucky because Ron could only see so many patients a day. By 8:00 a.m. every morning, the line of people who had walked up to 20 miles to be seen would be already too long. Sadly, many times half of the people had to walk back home with their pain.

This particular day, the 60-year-old Joyce was one of Ron's patients. She broke the record for the number of teeth pulled from one patient in a day: eight! I have no idea how she managed to walk back home but she did. After the teeth were pulled, I saw Joyce the following day in the market place. A much happier woman, she had this to say: "*The pain had been unbearable. I cannot thank the doctor enough for the pain and suffering that he saved me from. May God always bless him for his heart and the giving spirit that he demonstrated while treating us."*

What a Difference Fourteen Days Make!

Medical Vision Trips last no more than 14 days but they relieve the pain of a lifetime. Just imagine that. During those two weeks, members of the community receive basic medical services to address some of their health problems that have nagged these poor people for years. The doctors I have seen on our trips don't come to that part of Africa for a nice vacation. In fact, as Ron put it, these professionals could instead be taking nice vacations with 'umbrella drinks' and there is absolutely nothing wrong with that. Instead, they sacrifice those comforts to spent time with the needy that have nothing material to ever offer them. What a difference 14 days can make!

As I shared in an earlier chapter, since the summer of 2004, I have been privileged to lead many Vision Trips to Africa. Mostly, the teams have been comprised of pastors and ordinary Christians who love and want to serve God in these AIDS ravaged regions of the world. On these traditional Vision Trip teams, we do some speaking in churches, schools, home visits, and other things. Medical teams, however, have been fewer and farther between. What I have found instructive though is that whenever I go back to Africa without a team, people normally inquire about medical teams. The questions I get are usually along the lines of, *'When will the medical team come? When will those dentists return to help us?"* Rarely do I get asked, *'When will those pastors come back to preach to us?"* I must confess that as a preacher, the fact that they don't seem to miss preachers as much bothers me a little. However, I do understand where they are coming from. As Ron put it so aptly, dentists and doctors take the peoples pain right away. Yes, these folks need Christ because they want to end up in heaven and live for him today. However, right now, they are in pain and need some immediate, physical relief. It is truly incredible to talk to the community and feel the collective appreciation of the impact that medical teams make.

Living on Under $2 a Day

Short-term trip critics wonder whether it is really worthy it to travel 8000 miles for two weeks to do so little. Absolutely yes! Take the case of Joyce for example. As I talked with Joyce and reflected on her situation, what was impressive is not so much the number of teeth removed. That is significant enough because her pain was taken away. But even more important is that this was a service she could not otherwise afford on her own. Although removing a tooth in Kenya costs less than a mere three dollars, it is unattainable in a country where the average person lives on less than two dollars a day. It is not hard to see why Joyce could not afford the cost of removing eight teeth in other hospitals. Since we encourage partnership, Joyce paid a small fee (equivalent to 66 cents) for the entire service. Even among the poorest of the poor, people appreciate services better when they have contributed, however meager.

The more invasive operations undertaken by the Joshua International Medical Group each cost thousands of dollars. I remember visiting briefly with two elderly women at TIBA Medical Center in Nairobi where the operations were performed. They both admitted that without the intervention of the medical team from America, they would have suffered the rest of their lives because there was no way their respective families would ever afford the cost. To them, these operations were a dream come true.

Certainly, two weeks of work in a region of approximately 40,000 people- 90% of them without any form of health insurance and living in abject poverty- does not go very far. But the fact is that if some 700 people get help, then the community has 700 more people who are relatively healthier. I do not see ours as a call to eradicate all physical suffering, but to mitigate what we are able to as God provides partnerships. I see our work as a compliment to what other agencies and government health departments are already doing. Furthermore, our *searcher approach* is effective and immediate. The big *planners*—such as the respective governments, the G8, and others do not offer the sick the immediate help they need. In her lifetime, Joyce has attended numerous meetings where politicians promise all kinds of help to the poor but most of it is never delivered. In fact, she has reached a point where she doesn't care anymore what they say about the big plans to build bigger and better hospitals in coming years. She is concerned about having her pain removed *now*. That immediate help is the niche of short-term medical teams. They will never replace the long-term solutions that governments promise and sometimes deliver, but they are important complimentary services.

I will never forget what one elderly gentleman told a medical team working in a small village called Maweli in SE Kenya in summer 2007. After spending five days and seeing several hundred patients, Saturday came and we had to leave. However, there were still hundreds of patients waiting to be seen by the doctor and dentist on our team. When I told the people the bad news, one elderly gentleman who had been waiting on the line beckoned me. I said to myself, oh no, he must be mad with us. But instead, he stood up, thanked the team, and said, *"We are grateful that at least some of our people were attended to. We will come back next year."* I felt so bad that so many sick people who had walked from miles away with diseases that had ravaged them for years had to be told they could not be seen. I left feeling both grateful for all that had been accomplished but also feeling bad that these would have to wait for at least one more year. *'What if some don't make it another year'*, I thought to myself. As I watched the multitude leave, I was reminded of the starfish story, which goes something like this:

An old man walked along the shoreline. Up ahead, he could see that the tide had receded, leaving behind thousands of beached starfish as far as the eye could see. Stranded high upon the sand, the starfish seemed certain to perish. Near the water's edge, a young girl scurried back and forth, picking up the creatures one by one and throwing each gently back into the water. The old man approached her, overwhelmed at the apparent futility of the girl's task. "Why are you doing that?" He motioned toward the vast field of starfish stretching far into the distance. "There are too many of them! What can it possibly matter?" The little girl smiled and raised a single starfish high into the air before tossing it to safety. "It matters to this one," she said.[91]

Out of a population of 40,000 people, 700 were relieved of their pain during that 14-day visit! *It matters to Joyce* that eight teeth, which had bothered her for years, were finally removed. *It matters to the 15 patients* who had various operations done. Humanly speaking, there was no way these folks will ever get relief. Don't tell these folks those 14 days of treatment don't matter. It does matter to them.

Let's Look at the Big Picture

It is always important to put things into perspective. As I write this book, there is a big debate in America, the most advanced nation on earth, as to the direction that healthcare should take in the years to come. Most experts admit that the current healthcare system in the country is not working well for everyone. At least it is not working for the 45 million or so low-income and poor Americans who do not have health care coverage. But let's be real. Flawed as it may be the healthcare system in America is many times better than one finds in most developing nations. In fact, there is really nothing to compare when you consider the level of poverty one witnesses in the developing countries. I do not need to belabor the point since I have dealt with the matter of poverty in previous chapters. Suffice to say, I will highlight a few salient points here.

Three of the eight Millennium Development Goals (MDGs) agreed upon by the United Nations and pushed by the G8 are the reduction of child mortality, improvement of maternal health and combating of HIV/AIDS, malaria and other diseases.[92] These are all critical needs in poor countries. The question remains, how well are we doing nine years later? According to the available data, not as well as the launchers had hoped.

Preventable Diseases

Africa still suffers from preventable diseases that are a thing of the past in the developed world. Something as basic as immunization coverage has still not realized its potential, leaving millions of children unprotected and susceptible. Vaccine security is fundamental to meeting immunization goals and long-term funding remains a serious issue as neither developing country governments nor the international community has made firm commitments.[93] For example, access to vaccines for the six immunization-preventable diseases- namely, pertussis, childhood tuberculosis, tetanus, polio, measles and diphtheria is still a challenge for many developing countries. Malaria still kills millions every year in poor countries. The statistics for malaria are very depressing. For example, there was an estimated 247 million cases among 3.3 billion people at risk in 2006 causing death to nearly 1 million, mostly children under 5 years old. 109 countries were epidemic for malaria in 2008, 45 of them in Africa.[94] It is unfathomable that in the 21st century, 1 million people would die of a disease that most people don't even know still exists. The only time I think of malaria is when I travel to Africa. This disease has been eradicated in America.

Jesus' Mobile Medical Clinic

"Jesus traveled through all the towns and villages of that area, teaching in the synagogues and announcing the Good News of the Kingdom. And he healed every kind of disease and illness. When he saw the crowds, he had compassion on them because they were confused and helpless, like sheep without a shepherd. He said to his disciples, 'The harvest is great, but the workers are few. So pray to the Lord who is in charge of the harvest; ask him to send more workers into his fields." (Matthew 9:35-38 NLT)

I find this story relevant for at least two reasons. First, there is a lot of work to be done. It is eye opening to consider the events preceding these passionate words as recorded in Matthew. In 9:1-8, there is healing of a paralytic man. The calling of Matthew himself to join Jesus' ministry (9:9-13) follows this healing. We are then introduced to a stimulating discussion about fasting in 9:14-17. In 9:18-26, Matthew reports about the raising from death of a young girl and finally, in 9:27-34, we read about the healing of a blind man. Three out of these five cases involve healing, in one case, the raising of a dead girl back to life. I do not presume that Jesus healed or resurrected everyone he came across. It is, however, fair to state that he had compassion on such people and ministered to them regularly.

I don't intend to try and harmonize these events in a certain time frame and chronology since other Gospel writers give a slightly differing schedule from Matthew.[95] What is clear, however, is that regardless of the chronology of the events, this was a busy season for Jesus. Jesus immersed himself in the business of relieving people's pain, both spiritual and physical. What is not in doubt is that Jesus had come back from a preaching circuit and had witnessed the magnitude of what remained undone. It is incredible that Jesus being God would ask his disciples to pray for more workers. There is no question in my mind that Jesus had the authority to make a quick phone call or send an instant message to his father in heaven to have him send more troops. But, instead, he chose not to. He asked mere mortals, weak clay vessels to get involved in his work. I have thought many times why Jesus being God would want me involved in his work but I have never gotten a good answer. All I know is that he has asked me to go to the villages and demonstrate his compassion to the *Joyce's* of the world.

Second, it is important to recognize the urgency in Jesus' call. The twin use of the words 'sheep' and 'fields' connotes many, a big number. Considering the sheer numbers of people suffering today, Jesus' call is not only fresh but it is also urgent. Yes, the poor and the sick will always be with us. I believe that they still exist today so that Christian professionals can exercise their spiritual and natural talents to reduce the pain.

Tumaini Medical Clinic: A Drop in the Bucket?

In the previous chapter, I mentioned the two critical needs that the poor in Africa have talked to me repeatedly about: *healthcare* and *education.* To that end, we have sought partnerships in our child sponsorship program and in medical clinics. Through child sponsorship, we are able to provide access to formal education. We have also engaged in healthcare by building a medical clinic. The medical clinic was build to primarily provide for the needs of the AIDS orphans and their families and only secondarily as a service to the surrounding community. In reality, however, we have seen more patients coming from the community than anticipated. For example, between the months of May and September 2009, some 962 patients from the community went to the clinic as compared to only 183 AIDS orphans from our programs. The number is growing every month and we may soon be forced to expand the facility to enable us provide more services.

What I have noticed is that when Christian agencies answer the questions that the communities are asking, the results are immediate. Granted, this particular medical clinic is small and really a drop in a big bucket. However, what we are seeing is very promising. I am grateful to the partnership between Parkcrest Christian Church and others for making it possible to have the clinic. Small as it is, it has become a beacon of hope in a community of some 40,000 people. The staff consists of believers and the patients appreciate their servant leadership approach. I am grateful to both Kenyan donors who are locally contributing time and gifts-in-kind to ensure that the medical clinic is operational. I am also grateful for the partnership with Joshua International Medical Group and Dr. Ron Jurgensen for their frequent Vision Trips.

Through this small venture, God is teaching a lot of lessons. The one key lesson is that I should not be overwhelmed by the fact that nearly 1 million people die every year from malaria. I should not be overwhelmed by the fact that millions of poor people still die from the six preventable diseases. I should not just get mad and stay mad at the G8 or whoever is taking their precious time with talks about lofty political go-nowhere plans when the poor die from a lack of immunizations that cost 12 cents. Instead of putting all my energy into those negative thoughts, I want to focus on the positive things that God is already doing. Don't get me wrong. I know the Church has a prophetic role to play. We need to call out our respective governments whenever they cross the line. Some Christians may even be called to work in their governments. We have plenty of examples in the Bible—Nehemiah and Daniel, to name a few.

However, as a *searcher* I feel that Christian agencies and churches have a huge role to play in healthcare and other matters when it comes to global poverty. I am calling the Church to realize what we have on our hands. Jesus spent the bulk of his time doing stuff that needed to be done—like healing the sick, raising the dead and calling disciples to help in evangelizing the world. Why not just do the stuff that we have been called to do? The statistics I shared in this chapter are not just numbers. Behind each number is a real human being who was created in the image of God, just like you and me. What an opportune time for us to get up and do God's stuff.

Chapter 11

Church Plant:
The Indispensable Piece

Laretta

"...Your plans sound great and well thought out. ....The idea of having a New Testament church in Masii [Kenya] is exciting. ...We would not want to be singled out as benefactors, only guests. We do not want to give the impression that N. Americans bring Jesus and the money from the sale of his cattle on a thousand hills with us in our suitcases. We always intend to tie the nationals to the church, not to us. As you know, overall, the N. American church is rich materially but often

times poor spiritually. We find just the opposite in other countries. We don't want to ruin that. We benefit greatly from the example of faith and sacrifice we see in other countries where we partner. I too am excited since our goal is always to plant churches. Being part of planting one in Masii in addition to the adoption program [AIDS orphans] is a plus." [96]

This is an excerpt of an email exchange between me and Laretta in the spring of 2008. Our correspondence centered on the possibility for Tumaini partnering with First Christian Church in Yuma, Arizona to plant a church in Masii, Kenya. In October 2008, this partnership bore fruit and a church was planted. The name of the church is Masii Christian Chapel (MCC). Today, the church is growing and averaging 120 members every Sunday morning. Perhaps a little background is in order:

Can You Plant Just a Church For Us?

When the Lord laid a burden on my heart to work with AIDS orphans in Africa, I determined to take a non-denominational approach. I realized that the region we were working in was heavily denominational and most churches focused their social programs exclusively for their members. I understood the rationale but I wondered if that was necessarily the right way to go. Right from the onset, I sought to help orphans who were needy regardless of their religious backgrounds. I was very intentional in stating that the only qualification for the children to be helped was that they had lost one or both parents to the disease. I did not care whether the orphans came from Christian or non Christian families. I did not care whether they were from other organized religions or from animistic families. As it turned out, most of the orphans came from either non-believing families or families with nominal commitment to any religion or worship institutions in the area. That was back in late 2002 and early 2003.

A few years later, a number of people from the area came to us with a request. *"Can you plant just a church for the community?"* Having served as a pastor and professor in the area in previous years, I knew what they were asking. They wanted a simple, community church to serve their needs without denominational elements.

Historical Factors

I resonated with those who asked us to plant *just a church*. The issue of regional denominationalism is not unique to SE Kenya. In many parts of Africa, the Church is heavily denominational. This is no one's fault in particular. Indeed, the current church in Africa is a product of missionary comity decisions (the idea of missionaries dividing the land so that there is no overlap or fighting) that were made over a hundred years ago. Church historians have dealt with this matter at length and I do not intend to discuss it here. Suffice to say that today, for better or worse, African countries are divided according to deeply entrenched denominational lines. If there are any bad elements in the denominational model, the church in Africa is a victim of historical circumstances that are hard to reverse.

There are pros and cons in any of the church models one chooses to adopt. Those who support a strong, centralized, top-down approach of church polity point to the unity denominationalism bring to their congregants. On the other hand, those who favor a more congregational approach point to the New Testament churches as autonomous entities. From my experience, much of what we observe in Africa is a shift in focus. Instead of equipping the saints to do the work of ministry (Ephesians 4:11 ff), a lot of energy and resources are spent on serving the denominational hierarchy. Indeed, many church denominations have been caught up in serving the **organization** and there is almost no **organism** left in the body of Christ. I think that is why some cried out, *can you plant just a church where we can worship and serve God without the denominational yoke*.

As the years have gone by, I have continually sensed the prompting of the Holy Spirit in response to this need. I have no illusions that planting *just a church* is a ticket to a perfect church. Perfect churches don't exist because those of us who plant them and those who worship in them are not perfect. I am just grateful that God is allowing us an opportunity to plant an autonomous congregational church for the local community where they can learn about his love and salvation and serve him through others.

Perfect Timing

When it is time to take action, God normally brings many factors to converge. Taking time to pray and work on the logistics for a new church plant proved invaluable. Sharing the vision, need and opportunity with brothers and sisters was important. We have seen God orchestrate everything until it was time to take action. Within five years, God has enabled us to touch the lives of over 1000 orphans. About 70% of the children are not only poor orphans but also come from non-Christian backgrounds. They are not only economically forgotten but spiritually left behind as well. The rest come from nominal Christian backgrounds. It has not been a surprise to us that over 90% of the children have given their lives to Jesus as their Lord and savior during Christian camps. The timing was right. These statistics tally with what we find globally.

The Need for Christian Witness

It is gratifying to note that biblical faith is growing and spreading to the ends of the earth as never before.[97] What is even more encouraging is that "the percentage of Christians active in some form of mission today is at an all-time high of 36 percent"[98]. Indeed, according to Adherents.com, although Islam is the fastest growing religion, Christianity is still the largest religion with over 2.1 billion of the world religious followers[99].

Despite these obvious successes in Christian witness, however, there is still work to be done. The Great Commission remains an urgent command for all Christians considering that there are about 2 billion souls or 10,000 people groups yet to be reached with the gospel.[100] It is instructive to note that 95 percent of these unreached souls live in the 10/40 Window, a restricted part of the world with the majority of inhabitants being Muslim, Buddhist and Hindu people groups. For those of us who serve in developing countries, we can't ignore the fact that a very large proportion of those who have not heard the gospel are also materially poor. Indeed, 85 percent of the world's poorest countries lie within the unevangelized.[101]

Why it is Urgent to Plant Churches

The numbers of the unsaved speaks for itself. Human beings can only make the decision for Christ while they breathe. Once we are gone, we are gone. No matter what else we do as Christians, church planting must remain a priority. I think this is especially so in areas where we are involved in social programs.

In the summer of 2008, I attended a funeral for an 8 year old boy who had succumbed to AIDS. He was one of our sponsored orphans. His parents had died from AIDS and he was one of the unfortunate ones to be born with the virus. What made the ceremony particularly difficult was that the boy's grandmother was so sick the week the boy died that the family decided to not even let her know of his death and the funeral. She loved her grandson and they thought that informing her would only make her medical condition worse. When asked by the family's pastor to lead the eulogy, I read the story about King David's reaction after the death of a child. Here is what it says in part:

> *"His advisers were amazed. 'We don't understand you', they told him. While the child was still living, you wept and refused to eat. But now that the child is dead, you have stopped your mourning and are eating again. David replied, 'I fasted and cried while the child was alive, for I said, perhaps the Lord will be gracious and let the child live. But why should I fast when he is dead? Can I bring him back again? I will go to him one day, but he will not come back to me.'" 2 Samuel 12:21-23. NLT*

I like David's perspective on death. He knew that the life we live here on earth is temporary and a better life awaits those who love God. Indeed, if we picture eternity as presented in scriptures, we will quickly realize that those of us who are alive waiting to die are really not alive. Rather, as believers, we are dying waiting to live when we quit from these temporary shelters and spend eternity with the Lord. I think Jesse Jackson captured this thought very well when he said at a funeral that *"We act like life was certain and death uncertain. Life is uncertain and death is certain."*[102] Most of us don't think about death when we are in our prime. But death is a reality, whether we are 12 years old or 85 years old.

I have been thinking about death in the context of sub-Saharan Africa. This is the most death-prone region in the entire world. Elsewhere, I have tried to offer a macroeconomic picture of this region and shown how dire things are. According to World Health Organization (WHO), sub-Saharan Africa has one of the lowest life expectancies. Consider these statistics for example:

"The overall life expectancy in sub-Saharan Africa has dropped precipitously over the past 10 years, mostly because of the AIDS epidemic, the WHO says. Life expectancy dropped for female babies from 51.1 years to 46.3 years. For males, the level dropped from 47.3 years to 44.8 years. AIDS is now the leading cause of death in Sub-Saharan Africa, far surpassing the traditional deadly diseases of malaria, tuberculosis, pneumonia and diarrhea disease. AIDS killed 2.2 million Africans in 1999, versus 300,000 AIDS deaths 10 years previously."[103]

A more recent survey shows that while life expectancy has gone up globally, it has actually gone down in Africa:

"Average life expectancy at birth globally in 1995 was more than 65 years, an increase of about 3 years since 1985. It was over 75 years in developed countries, 64 years in developing countries, and 52 years in least developed countries. The world's lowest life expectancy at birth, just 40 years, is in Sierra Leone - barely half of the world's highest, in Japan, where it is 79.7 years. At least 18 countries in Africa have a life expectancy at birth of 50 years or less. The number of countries with a life expectancy at birth of over 60 years has increased from at least 98 (with a total population of 2.7 billion) in 1980 to at least 120 (with a total population of 4.9 billion) in 1995. On average, women today can expect to live over 4 years

longer than men - 67.2 years versus 63 years. The female advantage is greatest in Europe - almost 8 more years - and smallest in South-East Asia, where it is just one year." [104] *[Emphasis added].*

A few years ago while visiting family in Kenya I learned that a man I had known since he was a small boy had fallen seriously ill. One morning I went to his house to see how he was doing. On arrival, I was shocked to learn that although he had all classic symptoms of someone with AIDS-- had lost a lot of weight, had blisters all over his body, had TB and other respiratory problems making it difficult for him to breath or talk-- he had refused to take the HIV test. When I suggested to his wife and parents that they should take the dying man to the hospital, they were categorical. *"No, we don't treat witchcraft in hospitals. We have been to several witchdoctors and they have all told us exactly what is going on. Our son has been bewitched and we know who did it. You are welcome to pray but we are not taking him to the hospital."* A few days later, the man succumbed to his illness and died at the age of 35 leaving behind a widow and several children. As far as I know, no one in the family knew the Lord. The funeral was a gloomy ceremony and when the deceased's father rose to speak, he sobbed and decried the cruel hand of death that had taken their son at such a young age. He then asked a rhetorical question that has stayed with me ever since:

> *"Why is it that we are burying our children? This is not right. Children should bury their parents and not the other way round."*

The fact is, death is inevitable. As I continue to address the challenges brought about by HIV/AIDS, I am more convinced than ever before that church planting will need to be front and center of this holistic ministry. The children who have lost so much need to know about the love of God and the possibility of eternal life. The children who are HIV+ and possibly won't live for long need to know that their eminent physical death is not the end of life. The widows who are HIV+ need to know the Lord. The community members who are still in denial of the reality of HIV and AIDS need a savior who will change their world view and realize that HIV is not brought by witchcraft or mosquito bites but through sexual contacts, among other ways. The corrupt officials who feed the bottomless pit of greed at the expense of the poor need a savior to change their world view. The poor and the rich need a savior. Everyone needs an opportunity to hear the good news that God can accept them as they are through the shed blood of Jesus Christ. They need a place to worship as they serve the Lord who will be with them for the remainder of the few days left on earth and they need to know the eternal hope in Jesus.

Worth Pointing Out

Leading people to the Lord is a sure way of changing their life style. This in turn is a way of addressing the HIV/AIDS problem upstream. As the WHO show, there is a direct correlation between HIV/AIDS and low life expectancy in Africa. Without being too judgmental, I think it is fair to say that the core of this pandemic disease is sin! People need to know the Lord and begin leading a lifestyle that pleases him. Of course, there are several known ways through which people get infected with HIV—blood transfusion, sharing drug needles, at child birth, and breastfeeding—however, the majority of the infections in Africa are believed to be through unsafe sexual contact. I am aware of the socio-economic factors that drive the poor in the region to prostitution and the like. This is why the Church must simultaneously provide concrete programs that address those temporary but real needs as well. The point is that, if we don't address people's hearts we will have missed the mark.

Church planting that is holistic in nature is an answer to begin reversing these trends. Given the poverty context, church planting must address people's spiritual and physical needs. There is no way we can tell poor people to give their hearts to God, give us their little money in tithes and offerings and 'go home and be warm.' Yes we need to teach new believers to give and support God's work but if that is all we do with poor believers, the prospects for their survival is minimum. Planting and discipling a young autonomous church in Africa is an arduous exercise that requires intentionality.

Masii Christian Chapel (MCC)

MCC opened its doors on October 5th, 2008. Just a year later, the church is growing and vibrant. On August 5th, 2009, following a holistic evangelistic outreach in town, I received the following email from William, the church pastor. *"The whole event was beyond our imagination, and it still remains above our description. All I say is God planned it and God did it, may His name be glorified forever. Like the Psalmist said, not to us, O Lord, not to us but to God be the Glory because of His Love and faithfulness. All I remember is that MCC owned the event. Men, women, youths and children worked tirelessly. Brethren from Nrb [Nairobi], Athi-river, JKUAT, Scott, and Bomani attended. ...The occasion was graced by diverse people of the society. Pastors, brethren from other Churches, business people, leaders of the society, youths, children etc. I witnessed unity of the Church throughout the event. The soccer match attracted a large crowd. Praise God for the Drug Abuse talk that came forth right after the game. HIV & AIDS was addressed with people going for voluntary counseling and testing. Referrals were made to Machakos General Hospital. It was good hosting a worship service at the Market ground. Many people had access to a worship service even those taking beer in the pubs. Praise God that over 50 people gave their lives to Christ. People gave over Kshillings 20,000 ($280) to support the event. The story continues... I don't think Masii is the same again. Please remind all our partners in the US and those who pray for us to find sometime and give thanks."*

Obviously, this is a snapshot of a long journey before MCC matures to a healthy, growing church. But the reality is that lives are being changed. In fact, lives are being transformed. There is a high level of excitement and a real sense of ownership by the congregants. Because of the stigma associated with AIDS, it is not everyday that people come openly in the market place to be tested for HIV. It is not everyday drug addicts come in the open and seek help from the church. It is a new day in the area when ordinary Christians are empowered through Christ and taught that they do actually matter to God and that their opinions are important as they together build the church of Jesus Christ.

Because of the stigma associated with HIV/AIDS, many disease sufferers have stayed away from the Church in general. Indeed, many churches seem to avoid or not know what to do with AIDS victims. It doesn't make it any easier that many of the disease sufferers do not go public about it. MCC doesn't have the answer either, or at least not yet. All we know is that Christ died for these folks as well. What we know is that the Bible calls us to minister to the spiritually lost (Matthew 28:18-20), the poor (Deut. 15:11), widows and orphans (James 1: 27) as well as the strangers and aliens (Psalm 146:9). The church plant is an attempt to do just that. However, unless MCC takes a new approach of how to minister effectively to this sector of society it will be business as usual.

The events at the evangelistic outreach speak for themselves. We tried to reach the whole person. Spiritually, at least 50 souls were won to the Lord during that event. Physically, those who had symptoms for HIV were tested, counseled and referred to the relevant institutions to get further help. Those who have been enslaved by drugs were counseled and some were spiritually delivered from those entanglements. Again these are baby steps but are good pointers to the fact that God has prepared peoples' hearts and is calling us to walk in and credibly present the gospel. I firmly believe that if we put our hands in God's hands, God will accomplish his purposes through this new church plant in the days to come.

Geoffrey's Blogs

I read the following blog posted by Geoffrey Nighswonger. Geoffrey, a 21 year old young man from Long Beach, California spent six months interning with Tumaini and MCC in Kenya. In MCC, he served as the youth pastor. Here is what he said in a blog about his experience of reaching those in the fringes of society in Masii:

> *"July 4th, 2009. Sometimes we slap a fat label on people's foreheads depending on the sins they have committed. If you have fallen too far in our eyes then you get the "UNCLEAN" label. We look at someone's situation and instead of seeing that person as a child of God we take out our best thumping bible to smack them over the head with the word of God. We look at someone's sin and throw them off to the side because we can*

never use them and if we can't use them than God probably wouldn't want them either. ...There is a single mother who lives here in Masii and her story is the epitome of why we need to walk away from looking down on others and embrace them. She works as a bar maid. This career choice comes with little pay and unfortunately prostitution to offset the bills that serving alcohol doesn't cover. This woman is one of the many mothers that struggle to provide food each meal and her and her daughter struggle for food and rent. She has all of the symptoms of being HIV positive but refuses to gives into the fear of being positive and refuses to be tested. With little hope of bettering her situation and lacking uplifting and empowering words of positive friends, this woman was lured in by suicide... Her story was brought to our attention by her sister and, I know it sounds crazy but call us rebels, we decided to go talk with her. The fact that Christians were in her home loving her and praying for her instead of condemning or judging her BLEW HER MIND! After a few visitations she made the decision to live her life for Christ and suicide no longer held her captive. ...We are looking into helping her start her own business. A business that will wipe away the shame from her face and that she can be proud of. ...She has a huge smile on her face each time I see her and I know that she is filled with that inexpressible and glorious joy that can only come from God."

This blog illustrates the kind of people MCC is drawing and reaching out to. However, MCC cannot take full credit for this new development. I see it as a movement of the Holy Spirit and opening the eyes of the town dwellers to open their hearts to God. For some reason, the people who are social misfits and don't fit in any of the other six existing churches in town feel welcomed into MCC. Again, MCC's response is not unique. Jesus already set the example for us. For example, except for their socio-economic difference, the lady that Geoffrey talks about here is not unlike the one who came to see Jesus at Simon the Pharisee's home, as recorded in Luke 7:36-50. Both women were 'sinners' and it is instructive how Jesus accepted the woman with open arms in the face of disdain and unbelief, both from his host Simon and possibly his own disciples. When Jesus told the woman, "Your sins are forgiven" (7:48, NLT), he baffled everyone in attendance. But the point of the story is that there is no sin that Jesus can't forgive. He forgives even the most socially unacceptable sins such as the one these two women share, the one woman in Capernaum and the other is Masii.

God is calling us to plant church at such a momentous time and I do not want to miss what the Lord wants to do with and through us. What an opportunity to show God's love to a sector of society that does not experience love on a regular basis. What an opportunity for the bar maid who may be sick and dying to know that there is a savior who will take her home and live with her eternally. What an opportunity for MCC to start holistic ministries and offer these women alternative economic livelihood.

Here is another blog from Geoffrey:

> *"July 1, 2009. In times of despair, pain and destitution we tend to cling onto something. When the storms hit some of us grab on to our faith and don't let go, some turn to relationships and seek the comfort of others, some turn to solitary environments and some of us turn to our addictions... In a community in which the majority looks to their farms for their food and income, a drought is disastrous. With no fields to look to, no herds to tend to and very little money to be made countless men can be found from sun up till far past the sun sets in "Kosovo" drinking away the little money they have been able to acquire. This local brew is deadly...*
>
> *Why do they do it? Well we asked them. Stress seems to be a big factor, and understandably so. It seems like anyone in that situation would be stressed, imagine being a father and not being able to provide the most basic and essential need for your wife and children, stress is understandable. Idleness seems to be another big reason for spending their days in*

Kosovo. There is only so much that someone can do with a farm without rain or crops, after a while you run out of chores to do on a farm, they say that they have nothing better to do. Some have desperately attempted to attain acceptance and find that they can't get it anywhere but in Kosovo where you are welcomed with arms wide open regardless of how much money you have as long as you have a cup of the local brew in your hand.

Today we made our regular visit to Kosovo. We were met with a two familiar faces and it wasn't long before a nice sized group joined us. We made our rounds of visiting, praying, preaching and simply talking with the Kosovo fellows. William and I had smiles painted on our faces and the fellas' had a cup clenched in their hands. We ended up getting probably over twenty Kosovo regulars interested in starting a small Kosovo church. We have been going there every week and are now well known and liked, by most people not everyone yet. The men there trust us and are very thankful of our going out of the way to see them. .... They have been mocked, laughed at, judged, condemned and ridiculed and now they have an opportunity to move past all of that. I think that the reason they are so adamant and excited about starting this ministry is because they wont be judged, instead they will be helped (we are going to be working on a rehabilitation program for some of the addicts that want help)."

Like the case of the bar maid, I have been encouraged to see how open the guys of Kosovo are to the gospel. But I also know that for some of them, this is not the first time they have heard the gospel. For some of them, they feel that the church has actually failed them. They feel that the church in general has only condemned them and never loved and shown them the right way

I saw this underlying anger at a funeral in the fall 2009 when I attended the funeral of one of the Kosovo men. This one man was a recent convert through the ministry of MCC and was regularly attending church. However, he died suddenly under very mysterious circumstances. The town was abuzz with speculation. Some said he had committed suicide while others said it was a case of homicide. The local government authorities were still doing investigation at the time of the funeral. At the funeral, the presiding pastor mentioned something about the ills of drinking during his sermon and the response from the Kosovo men was fast and furious. Yes, they know their need for God and rehabilitation but anytime Christians talk about their lifestyle in public, they get very agitated. In general, however, it seems that these men feel that there is a higher level of acceptance and sincerity in the way they have been approached this time round.

For every one bar maid or prostitute saved from suicide and shown God's unconditional love, it is a battle won. For every one prostitute who turns to God and with a little hand-up is able to start a new economic lifestyle, it is a battle won. For every Kosovo man who is challenged to re-think his priorities it is a step in the right direction.

What Kind of Churches Are Needed

The response at the evangelistic outreach, the bar maid's and the Kosovo men's response to the gospel leads me to ask the question, what kind of churches do we need in reaching this population? In a sense, this is not a new question. It is a question that all church planters must ask whenever they move to a new people group whether that be ethnic, racial, social, economic or otherwise. Jesus began his ministry where his recipients were. In church planting we do well to follow his example.

In the context of Masii, which is a microcosm of African towns and cities, we are confronted with several challenges: sin, abject poverty, 40%-60% unemployment, prolonged drought, entrenched traditional beliefs in witchcraft and other animistic practices, prevalence of HIV/AIDS and other health issues and heavy denominationalism, among other challenges. These realities must then inform the kinds of churches that we will need to plant to begin addressing some of these issues. As stated already, there is no attempt to plant perfect churches here. But we do want to plant **healthy** churches.

Spiritually Healthy

First and foremost, we want to plant churches where people can be presented the plan of salvation. A church is not a social club where people are invited to just feel good about themselves. No. The church was bought with the blood of Jesus Christ and this must be central to what we do. More importantly, we need to remember that this is a message of love and hope and needs to be presented in like manner. Pastors and other church leaders need to know that they are not CEOs who sit in some fancy offices waiting to be served. This top-down model is the exact opposite of the model we see in the scriptures. The folks we serve in African villages and big towns alike have seen enough of this top-down model in many churches and wonder whether there is a difference between church and secular leadership.

It is instructive to note that the bar maid mentioned in Geoffrey's blog was surrounded by six churches for many years but it wasn't until some ordinary Christians took the initiative *to go to her house* and show love she that decided not to take her life and began to open up to the possibilities of Jesus as an alternative. It wasn't until William and Geoffrey actually *visited Kosovo* that the men there began to look at church differently. We know that among those men who have accepted Christ, at least one of them came to church and although he didn't live long thereafter, he is with Jesus forevermore. These few examples tell us there is something to be said about following Jesus' example of humility and servant leadership. Although he was God, he became human and demonstrated uncommon love by coming down to where we live. Paul articulates this powerful imagery the best in Philippians 2:3-8 (NLT): *"You must have the same attitude that Jesus Christ had. Though he was God he did not think of equality with God as something to cling to. Instead he gave up his divine privileges; he took the humble position of a slave and was born as a human being. When he appeared in human form, he humbled himself in obedience to God and died a criminal's death on the cross."*

Mentally Healthy

In Masii and in the African context at large, the gospel of Jesus Christ must be presented in such a way that it addresses deep level world view issues. The family I introduced earlier in this chapter watched their loved one die from AIDS because they believed he was "bewitched". This incidence illustrates not just the lack of medical knowledge of connecting HIV to AIDS. It is much deeper than that. It illustrates a world view gap between the claims of the gospel and the deep level of allegiance to the gods that are believed to hover in the entire environment. The beliefs in spirituality and power (not Godly spirituality or power) is incredible in this part of sub-Saharan Africa. For this family, therefore, the gospel needs to be presented a little differently than it was presented, say, to Nicodemus in John 3. In fact, the powerful encounter recorded in 1 Kings 18 between the prophet Elijah and the prophets of Baal on Mount Carmel might actually speak to them better. Not because the analogy of the wind and the Holy Spirit that Jesus used with Nicodemus is irrelevant but because growing up in a drought prone area and in that spiritual environment, they can relate to the issues of spiritual power more easily. They can relate to a powerful God who brings rains more so than to a theoretical or cerebral explanation of the gospel. In a previous chapter, I talked about reaching the lost at three different levels-- their thinking (cognitive), their feelings (affective) and their values (evaluative). This is a long process but a necessary one if we are going to plant churches that are transformative. Africans are incredibly spiritual but we need to point them to a life-saving spirituality.

Socially & Physically Healthy

People on the fringes both economically and socially need a unique approach. Realistically, we are talking about a population that earns less than a dollar a day to feed themselves and their families. Because of the choices some of them have made in the past, some of these folks have big families to support and many times they feel hopeless and find it easier to simply prostitute themselves and unfortunately contract AIDS in the process. In the case of some men, they drink in order to 'forget' their problems but some end up dying in the process. These are deeply entrenched problems that need long-term solutions. Given the context, well planned recovery ministries as well as alternative economic options must be part of the equation. In these two areas—recovery programs and economic options—are the ones where the church in sub-Saharan Africa will need to partner with the western church because the latter has dealt with some of these addiction and micro finance issues for many years in the inner cities and have well-developed recovery programs that can be easily contextualized to meet African needs. After all, following the **wa kwetu** concept, the church is one big family of God and these are easy ideas to implement, especially in the 21st century with our advanced modes of communication and unbelievable technology.

In a word, I am calling for a holistic approach to church planting in Masii and other similar towns and cities across sub-Saharan Africa. MCC and other chapels that we will plant in the future have a special ministry niche. We serve a population that needs help in spiritual and other critically important aspects of their lives. Going forward, we must not only love the down-trodden and reach them where they are at. We must not just humble ourselves and love the sinners. We must also design recovery programs that address people at their world view levels. We must initiate income generating projects as an alternative to bar tending and other such occupations that do not bring honor to God's name. We must design rehabilitation programs to help the men from Kosovo begin to realize that there are other ways of dealing with poverty than the escapism that they have resorted to. We must continue to provide opportunities for those who are tired of a heavy denominational yoke to participate in congregations where they can have an immediate impact in their towns and beyond. As Bryant Myers put it so eloquently, *"People are whole beings--body, mind and social, intertwined in a seamless way. People are not disembodied souls nor spiritless bodies. Furthermore, they live in communities that are physical, social and spiritual."* [105]

Stanley M. Mutunga

Chapter 12

Sustainability:
Who's Defining?

Vickie

"We are into our second phase of our WEEP (Women's Empowerment Equality Project) program. Of the 53 women who have graduated from WEEP since 2005, we have identified some of them to head our new program. The new program is called Parents Rescue & Orphanage Prevention Strategy (PROPS). We have hired one of the WEEP alumni to head this training program. Sue is training other HIV positive

women on skills that they can utilize to get themselves out of poverty and support their families. I am extremely grateful to God for this accomplishment. I remember the time when Sue was on her deathbed. Today, she is not only strong but has a profession to actually be a teacher. Only God is able to make this possible.106" ~Vickie Winkler, HEART

Earlier in the book, I explained the distinction that William Easterly has given between the big organizations such as governments and the like versus smaller organizations. The former he called the *planners* and the latter, the *searchers*. I have been very impressed with the searcher mentality that Vickie Winkler of HEART has taken over the years. Starting the WEEP project with 5 AIDS women in 2005 that were on their death beds and to see the number grow to 53 within 4 years is a huge accomplishment. In a continent where thousands of AIDS widows die every day alone, this is a huge for the few that get help. It is certainly a step in the right direction.

TAA
Tumaini Alumni Alliance is a group of young adults consisting of current and alumni Tumaini children who have decided to minister to the poorest of the poor in their communities. As they say in their manifesto, they just want to extend the love and care that was given to them. They remember where they were before sponsorship and how far God has brought them. TAA has a clear vision, mission, goals and objectives that they want to realize in the months and years to come. In December 2008, seven of their members traveled ten miles from Masii, our headquarters, to visit one of the poorest families in the area. The Kivai family is comprised of four orphans-- two brothers and two sisters. They lost their single mother four years earlier and as is often the case, the children were left under the care of a poor grandmother, Anna Kataa Kivai. At the time of their visit, the two younger children, Mwendwa, an 11 year old boy and Sabina, his 5 year old sister were sponsored. Since then, the other two older children have been sponsored as well.

The family lives on a 2 acre piece of land and for the last 3 years, they have not had any rains. Consequently, food was difficult before the orphans got sponsored. Like other poor families in the area, the Kivai's live in a small grass thatched house. The family keeps two goats and that is really all they have in material wealth.

This particular day, the TAA members had raised some $33 among themselves (a tremendous amount comparatively) to buy Christmas gifts for the Kivai family. They also met another very practical need for that family. The family had no chairs, so the group came prepared to make temporary wooden benches outside their main house—thatched and all. It was an incredibly touching demonstration of love from a group of Tumaini students whose only desire was to bless others as they had been blessed.

> *"We are an inspired generation from Tumaini International Organization [Ministry]. We have started this [Tumaini Alumni Alliance] because of how our lives have been impacted. We have been helped and supported by people we do not even know and that are mainly what has touched us. .....we want to extend the same to other people and share with them the love of Jesus Christ. We thought this was one way of extending our heartfelt gratitude to everyone that has contributed to the success of Tumaini. We want to help and give people hope as well as draw them to Jesus Christ. We are driven by a strong force....we are determined to make a difference not only in the [our] society but also world wide."[107]*

When the Poor Gets it!

The actions of the TAA group has been a great encouragement to me. Knowing that the little that they have done so far, there may be hope for Africa in the up coming generation. In fact, the formation of TAA epitomizes what I hope and pray God is doing in the hearts of young Christians in Africa who are benefactors of various charity organizations. Thinking about their act of love and generosity in relationship to their own poverty conditions, I was reminded of a phrase I read somewhere that the best way to forget your own problems is to help someone else solve theirs.

When I interviewed some of the TAA members about their ministry to the Kivai family, I realized that it was actually a life-changing experience for some of them. For example, Lazarus observed that this was his first mission and *"Honestly we are meant to do this. If we can make people be as happy as Kivai's family, then I am willing to go all the way. I am proud of TAA and with God's power we will change many more lives."* Sylvester added, *"I was challenged by the hope and optimism that I saw in Mwendwa's eyes. The fact that an 11 year old boy could be this hopeful in the midst of such poverty blew me away. I found myself asking, why I wouldn't be as hopeful as he was."* And Judy said, *"To me, the mission was more than a challenge. Stepping into that home made me realize how hard I want to work and help many needy people. It empowered my sense of direction and showed me a picture of how life looked like. Honestly, my desire to help needy people grew then more than any other time of my life."*

When the poor are moved 'by the things that move the heart of God' and begin to realize that there are poorer people in their midst, it a first step toward the right direction. It is a first step toward economic sustainability. I believe that if Africa is going to begin to limp, not even walk, towards economic sustainability, it will have to begin with those who have tasted the goodness of the Lord through others. The TAA youth are a good example for others to follow. As already observed the levels of corruption and greed among most of the continent's current leadership is beyond description. I seriously believe that our long-term economic hope lies in developing a new crop of leadership that is both well educated and have an appreciation of a Godly worldview. This is the time to inculcate godly values so that they can appreciate the plight of the forgotten lot in their respective countries and do the right thing.

I believe if we can succeed in sustaining the fire in Lazarus, Sylvester, Judy and others like them we will have started well the long journey to sustainability. Changed lives—in a holistic sense—is the only hope for changing Africa.

A Common Misconception

Before we can delve further into the discussion of sustainability, I want to speak briefly to a common misconception. Many well-meaning Christians and, especially charity givers, view the poor as empty containers needing to be filled with goodies. When we take this view, we go to them based on our perception of *needs* and *wants.* Intentionally or not, we prescribe to the poor what we think they need, when they need it and how we will deliver what we think they need. The truth is, even the poorest of the poor know how to survive, and otherwise they would have been out of existence before our arrival. If we take the latter view, our helping them will take a different angle. We will go to them only as partners and ask them the question, *'how can I come alongside to work with you as you address your socio-economic situation?'* With this approach, they will know that we are not taking over their responsibilities. We are only coming alongside and offering a hand-up. Ultimately, it is their responsibility to address their own challenges, but we recognize a godly call to come alongside.

As I often tell our recipients, our partnership is not forever. It is only for a season. When the TAA team raised $33 dollars and came alongside the Kivai family, that great gesture didn't solve all the family's problems. The fact is the Kivai family already knew how to exist. The food and gifts helped them to live better. The sponsorship of the children has now made it possible for them to have school uniforms and fees taken care of. But the funds are not enough to move the family to another socio-economic class. The family will probably never live in a western style home, but it is good to work with them to build a better hut. The job of the Christian agency is to come alongside and create an environment—usually through healthcare and education--- for the family to be better able to move up the economic ladder, but that is not always the end result.

If we take this view of development, then sustainability becomes rather seamless. Since the poor already have some semblance of economic survival even before we come in, we endeavor to make very few changes in their lives so that they can do well when we are gone. If we don't try to make them live like us in the course of our helping them, they will be just fine when we are gone.

Let's consider a couple technical definitions of the term sustainability. The World Bank has defined sustainability as *"the capacity of a project to continue to deliver its intended benefits over a long period of time"*[108] Similarly, the USAID has viewed it more comprehensively as *"the ability of a program to deliver an appropriate level of benefits for an extended period of time after major financial, managerial, and technical assistance from an external donor is terminated"* [109] In both definitions, the underlying idea seems to be the <u>ability to continue</u> for an extended period of time.

I agree with the observation that, *"there may be as many definitions of sustainability and sustainable development as there are groups trying to define it. All definitions have to do with: living within the limits; understanding the interconnections among economy, society and environment; and equitable distribution of resources and opportunities.*[110]

I think that as long as one understands the basic cultural and socio-economic parameters, sustainability can be an elastic term dictated by the local context where it is applied. I think Peter Bardaglio said it best when he observed that, *"sustainability is not a product but rather an ongoing process <u>with no endpoint</u>."*[111]

Sustainability and Christian Development

Bryant Myers has provided perhaps the most comprehensive definition of sustainability in the context of transformational development. He points out that for a Christian agency to say that they have accomplished sustainability in a community, the latter must be sustainable in four areas: *physical* (provision of basic necessities: food, water, heath, economics, and environment), *mental* (intentionally address the deep-seated poverty of being or ontological poverty), *social* (return of some level of control of local resources), and *spiritual* (the realization that the community doesn't depend on donors but on God—attainment of a spiritual worldview).[112]

When I think of sustainability, these four words are my guiding principles. I think of *process* but not an *end product* in all the four areas. The church of Jesus Christ is an interdependent body and not independent institutions. The Church is first an organism and secondarily an organization for the purposes of fulfilling the Great Commission.

Because of my belief that sustainability stands or falls depending on one's spirituality, I want to highlight the *spiritual* component as the pillar where the rest of the pillars— physical, mental, and social aspects of sustainability must hold. Corruption, ineptitude and poor leadership in Africa cannot be corrected simply by giving more food and weaponry. Changing of worldview from that of culture of poverty to 'we can do it' alone will not help as that has been tried elsewhere with devastating results. If it were so, modernity would have solved all the world's problems. Social empowerment alone is not the solution either. More education on democracy, human rights and gender equality are all good topics to cover, especially in a continent like Africa where male chauvinism reigns. This alone is, however, not good enough.

Sustainability must of necessity be grounded on spirituality. At the end of the day, what I want to see in this unfolding process is that we are changing a generation that will affect Africa in way never seen before in all the four major areas with spirituality being foundational.

Key Ministry Components

When we think of sustainability in terms of *sustainable development*, we must also identify some key ministry components. All the three Christian agencies in this study have some version of local and overseas support for their work in rural areas and the urban slums.

We know that Community Transformers offers small-medium loans to HIV+ widows. They also sponsor various youth programs to get them out of drugs and gang activities. As we have seen HEART has an excellent WEEP program that helps HIV+ mothers stay alive and healthy to thus prevent more children from becoming orphans. Tumaini offers a child sponsorship program as well as micro-finance projects. I want to take a closer look now at some of these key ministry components: child sponsorship, People Overcoming Poverty, and micro-finance projects.

Child Sponsorship: "Kay"

"Tumaini loves me and has been my mother since she passed away. When I was completely hopeless with nowhere to go for guidance in live, Tumaini heard about my story and sought me. I am so glad they found me and completely changed my life."

Those were the opening words when I sat down with Kay, a Tumaini alumnus who now works as a hair dresser. Interviewing her in the spring 2009, this 21 year old girl demonstrated wisdom beyond her years. When her divorced mother died, Kay and her three siblings were left with no one to take care of them. Their grand parents who would have naturally taken them in had also died. Kay and her younger brother were taken in by an aunt while her two elder siblings went to look for manual labor jobs to provide food. However, that was just the beginning of their trouble. After about a year, Kay was kicked out of the house by the aunt. This happened to be her final year in elementary school and made it very difficult for Kay to continue with her education. In fact, Kay was homeless for months as a teenager. By God's grace, a neighbor had pity on her and agreed to house her until she could complete 8th grade, at which point she would move out to look for a job. Following her graduation from the 8th grade, Kay was homeless for a whole year, staying with a friend here and a friend there. Then Tumaini discovered her in the spring of 2005. Well, she came to Tumaini with incredible zeal and determination to succeed. Because of her age, she skipped high school and went straight to a vocational school to train as a hair dresser. Despite her educational level, she excelled in the program and graduated at the top of her class in 2007.

Kay has since found employment as a hair dresser. The business owner describes her as a model employee. She has accepted Christ into her life and has become a reliable counselor of young orphans going through what she did when her mother died. Kay's goal in the next couple years is to establish her own hair dressing business. She also wants to purchase land and build a house for her and her siblings. Listening to her and knowing how far she has come, there is no doubt in my mind that Kay will realize her goals and more. To say that she is a resilient woman is an understatement.

I am grateful for the long history of the western church and their giving to alleviate the needs of the developing world. Without hundreds of sponsors from America, many ministries would not be where they are today. But I would like to change that picture. For many years, child sponsorship was something that was associated with western assistance only. A cursory look at the way church work was supported mainly from the West will tell the full story. Africans were primarily recipients of charity and it never occurred to us that at one time we would be called upon to give to charity. This is the mold we are trying to break. We have experienced modest success, but I believe more ought to be done.

I know it is hard to remove a long standing history. But part of sustainability is to get more Africans involved in support charity agencies. What we are succeeding in doing is convincing a growing number of able Africans that we need to work together with the world community in addressing African problems. Community Transformers, for example, is doing a great job in garnering local support. In fact, it is high time that more Africans not only helped their own but also thought about the needs of the less fortunate in other countries, such as America—the inner cities of America, and the poor Appalachian communities, just to name a few. This is the mindset we must inculcate, especially among world Christians.

People Overcoming Poverty

The pilot project underway is changing the lives of five women and their families profoundly. Sustainability, being a process, will not be realized overnight. However, already the women's mind sets have been changed. They now know that some of their perennial economic challenges will be a thing of the past. Economic improvement positively affects one's social status. They know that the Christian agency involved only came in because of Jesus Christ. They have been given an opportunity to know Christ and make him known in their families, community and business environment. When will complete sustainable development be realized by these five women? I don't know but that is not important either. I am not worried about the endpoint. I only care that the process is going as it should. I am ok if they make a few mistakes and learn along the process. After all, these five women already knew how to survive even before we came in. We have given a hand-up and hopefully an environment for them to succeed in but it is completely up to them to define how the drama will end. This takes away the burden of sustainability from the Christian agency and shares the responsibility with the poor.

Micro-finance Projects

In July 2007 Tumaini launched a pilot micro-finance project in a small village called Kingatuani in SE Kenya. The $5,000 for the project was donated by Valley Christian Church in Chino, California. The recipients were a group comprised of 21 members with funding distributed into 6 different businesses: Dairy farming, Retail shops, Cereal crops, Green vegetables, Nursery tree planting, and Livestock trading. The amounts of the loans were allocated according to the nature of business. Everyone was given a grace period to repay their loans, again based on the nature of business undertaken.

The reason why this particular group was selected was because the members were already trying to address their own problems. This was a critical benchmark on which the amount of the loan was decided. Those who had higher stock/capital and business experience/success got slightly higher loans. When I interviewed the members before the launch, virtually all the applicants indicated that they wanted to double or triple their business profit margins at the end of the project.

Within a period of one year, about 50% of the borrowers had realized their goals. A couple of them did extremely well. Others did not triple or double their businesses as they hoped due to a variety of variables including drought, thefts, sickness and a competitive market that made it hard for them to reach their targeted goals. We had only one outstanding defaulter.

This partnership between Tumaini and Valley Christian Church was meant to assist the poor who were already addressing their own socio-economic challenges. We were very intentional in introducing Christ in the mix. The group met weekly for devotions because we felt spirituality must be foundational in all they did. The funding helped alleviate their economic and social issues. In the process, their worldview was addressed—they were empowered to realize that solutions to their challenges lay in their hands. The international and local Christian communities came alongside give a hand but not to take over their lives.

Have these folks reached sustainability? Perhaps not all of them have. However, we were instrumental in helping them start the journey. Sometimes that is all God asks us to do---to be a channel of blessing to someone poor in a certain season in their lives. A few times in the gospels we see Jesus feeding the hungry, and healing the sick of all manner of disease. Jesus did not rid the communities of all their hunger and disease. He did, however, set up an excellent example of compassion.

Sustainability vs. Dependency

If we agree that sustainability entails *"the ability of a program to deliver an appropriate level of benefits for an extended period of time after major financial, managerial, and technical assistance from an external donor is terminated,"* as USAID put it, then one of the responsibilities of charity organizations is to intentionally do things that will help accomplish that goal. Sustainability is a process without an endpoint. However, that does not mean that the poor should perennially rely on the non-poor for their material upkeep. Based on the ministry contexts, local support must be sought at all times so that unhealthy dependency does not occur.

It is important to acknowledge that the issue of sustainable development is not always a clear cut issue. This is especially so when we push self-reliance as a goal rather than a long, arduous process. The Church by its very nature is a body—a body composed of different members (1 Corinthians 12). In other words, the church of Jesus Christ is an interdependent institution. Some members of the body of Jesus Christ are non-poor; some are poor and others in between. Some members of the body live in Asia; others live in Africa, some in Europe, Australia, America and South America. When Jesus taught and demonstrated love for his Church, he did not put any physical boundaries on who a neighbor is. In the story of the Good Samaritan, for example, the Samaritan did not limit his help. Instead, he offered to pay the owner of the hotel all the expenses incurred by the injured man as long as the man needed help. This is how Luke put it. *"The next day he handed the inner keeper two silver coins, telling him, 'Take care of this man. If his bill runs higher than this, I'll pay you the next time I'm here" (Luke 10:35 NLT).*

I wonder, what does this say about our artificial end-points for the various projects—child sponsorship, micro-finance endeavors, among others—that we operate. I do not think the implication in this story is that we should help the poor perennially; but I also think that we need to be careful that we don't simply follow the bandwagon of self-reliance blindly at the expense of God's intentions for given individuals and communities. We need to balance compassion which could easily lead to dependency syndrome with the need for sustainability. We also need to remember that once we have given the poor a hand-up, they need to heed God's call to work. The apostle Paul had this to say to the church at Thessalonica. *"Even while we were with you, we gave you this command, 'Those unwilling to work will not get to eat" (2 Thessalonians 3:10 NLT).* This is where the Church needs to work closely with the recipient communities and keenly listen to the inner voice of the Holy Spirit. The danger is either to stay too long or to leave too early.

Chapter 13:

What Could God Be Saying?

Remember Them?

Throughout this book, I have introduced you to several of God's ordinary but resilient people. These people have impacted me in ways that I will never forget for the remainder of my days on earth. These men and women, boys and girls are the reason for this book.

I have introduced you to young children such as Muli and to young men and women with varied backgrounds. Among these are Joey, Grace, Julie, Lois and Liz, who though traumatized after losing their parents, have shown zeal and determination to make life work for them and those around them. I introduced you to a very special young man, Julius. His change of heart that allowed him to forgive family members serves as an example of the depth of change that Jesus is bringing in the lives of young men and women in Africa. I introduced you to Mo, John, and Cox and we saw what education has offered them. I introduced you to a few women in the slums of Nairobi: Teca, Fatuma, Nora and Christie, as examples of how God through the acts of ordinary Christians has brought the dying back to functional living. What a God we serve! I introduced you to several grandmothers, among them the enterprising Ruth in the slums of Nairobi and Milcah in the Masii area. What a resilient team of grandmothers doing everything they can to raise their grandchildren under the harshest of circumstances. I introduced you to ordinary Christians like Mike a.k.a. "Mwau" whose testimony of incredible loss of family and recovery from drugs led some 50 Tumaini kids to change their lives in one night. I introduced you to some incredible pastors such as Kerry, Jim, Laretta, Mike and Roger, whose leadership led entire congregations to take steps to change the course of their congregations and hundreds of AIDS orphans and widows in Africa. I introduced you to my amazing friend and co-worker in Kenya, Vickie. Vickie is simply an amazing widow who answered the call to move to Africa, resulting in the founding of HEART and now HIV+ women have found a second chance to live.

Who will forget Rick, the 26 year old orphan raised by a drug addict in one of the largest slums of Africa, the Mathare slums? After giving his life to Christ, Rick ended up founding Community Transformers and is now turning hundreds of youths to Christ and a new beginning.

Who will forget Mutish! A boy who by his own admission was fast becoming a local thug in his town of Masii until he found hope through Tumaini. He is now studying to become a missionary doctor! Who will forget Biko, a teenage boy whose faith in Jesus and a high school education saved his family's farm from greedy government officials?

Who will forget the story of Jack's experience on a vision trip when he was touched by the level of poverty after visiting a family in Africa to the point of leaving his own shirt behind? Who will forget the story of Ashley who on the same trip was touched by the grandmother's poverty situation she left behind the only thing she had—her shoes? Who will forget Dr. Ron's testimony about his dentistry work in Africa and how that means much more than taking an expensive vacation? I can go on and on.

There is one common denominator in all these stories. The stories begin and end with the love of God. Yes, some of these people show faith, hope and resilience in the most difficult of circumstances. But in each situation, God is bringing his people, both the poor and the non-poor to intersect in various situations and the result is that lives are being changed. God is bringing his people to encounter orphans, widows and grandparents who had been forgotten and is using them to bring hope. The question now is, *what could God be saying to you through these stories of hope, faith and resilience?*

I Am Humbled

On October 10th, 2001, I held a meeting with my founding board of directors and shared my vision with them. I told them how God had tugged on my heart to stand with AIDS orphans in Africa. I told them that my BIG DREAM was to see us partner with 3 churches, build a multi-purpose community center and provide support for 250 orphans by 2011. We spent some time in prayer and left.

God has more than answered that prayer. I have been humbled, not only by the number of ministry partners that God has brought our way, but more so by the various ways he has made the connections. Truly, God is not a God of conventional ways. As I write this book, we have tripled the number of children that we serve. We have more than ten churches in partnership. More importantly, Tumaini International Ministries does not stand alone in the ministry to AIDS orphans and widows. As I have stated throughout the book, I have been both blessed and challenged by other equally effective grassroots Christian agencies.

But there are still millions of AIDS orphans and widows who remain forgotten in Africa, Asia, America, South America and Europe. God loves each and every one of those folks. I like Bob Robert's earlier call for Transformed Lives and Transformed World. He says that if our lives are transformed, we will begin viewing the whole world differently. In his case, he had to make vision trips around the globe for God to touch him with the needs of the world. I am not suggesting that every Christian must make vision trips all over the world over to appreciate these needs, although some will need to. No, God can speak to us no matter where we are. Just ask the biblical Moses, Gideon, and Jonah, among others. What I am saying is that given the human statistics that I have covered in this book and the number of unprecedented opportunities to serve all over the world, I am challenging you to ask these questions:

> *What could God be saying to me as an individual? What could God be saying to us as a family? What could God be saying to us as a church? What could God be saying to us a Christian university? What could God be saying to us as a denomination?*

In Their Own Words

I want to share several testimonials of some who have asked themselves the question, *what could God be saying* in the wake of this unprecedented epidemic. These Christian leaders not only asked themselves the question but also participated on one of or more vision trips to Africa to see for themselves what God was already doing and in the process found their ministry niche.

> *"I am proud of the partnership that Parkcrest has developed with Tumaini International Ministries, because how the Church responds to the HIV/AIDS pandemic is a significant call that God has placed on our generation. Tumaini provides an accessible onramp for anyone to be able to make a difference for at least one child in Kenya. Their work is significant and their ministry is one that can be trusted."*
> *~Mike Goldsworthy*[113]

> *"I love the work of Tumaini, and I love the kids that this mission serves. By getting involved with Tumaini, our church has discovered in a very practical way what Jesus meant when he said, "It is more blessed to give than to receive." Let the people in your church discover the joy of being 'world changers' one life at a time." ~Kerry Decker*[114]

*"Being involved with Tumaini has been an incredible blessing to First Christian Church, Yuma, AZ. Sixteen of us have had the opportunity to visit Kenya and over 100 children are being sponsored by people connected to FCC somehow. .....It has made the pandemic, so far way, come close to us. ...Our small groups wait for letters from their child while faithfully praying for them each time they meet. And it is those letters that tug at our heartstrings. To be called Mum and Dad by children most have never met, to begin to comprehend that $30 a month may mean one less meal in a restaurant for us but it means **life** to a child in Kenya is indeed life changing. One young man who traveled with the 2007 team came back and planted 10 acres of wheat and gave the profits to Tumaini. This same man stood in front of the church, the Sunday after he returned from Kenya, and wept over what he had seen. I have heard over and over from our sponsors that everything they spend is now measured against what $30 will do for a child in Kenya. It has been a reminder to us that Jesus said, "The Spirit of the Lord is on me, because he has anointed me to preach good news to the poor..." ~Laretta Shrader*[115]

"Our church involvement with Tumaini *birthed out of Dr.* Mutunga's *friendship and investment in my education at HIU, as he communicated a desire to bring hope to HIV/AIDS victims in Kenya. So, in 2007, we began a pilot project to assist needy families with small loans to begin or expand a business in order to provide subsistence income. Valley Christian Church adopted a small village and, in the process, made lifelong friends and partnerships within that small community. We ventured far from Southern California on a vision trip – not only to begin the micro-enterprise effort – but to see if in fact the ministry was "the real deal." Not only did our small team confirm it visibly, but our entire congregation saw the blessing of investing in people who are deeply loved by God. Through this outreach and a few dozen child sponsorships, the world*

became smaller and closer to us. Over the next year as we interacted with our "kids," this partnership renewed our call to mission. We sensed God's prompting to return with a team of 17, over half from our youth group, to spread the love of Christ through community outreach, VBS, and home visitations. Our faith has been tested and refined in sending two teams, and true discipleship has been the result. Yes, the Church has done wonders at throwing money at various charities, but I cannot emphasize enough the value of touching lives, one-on-one, to communicate to a region ravaged by death, disease and poverty that they are <u>not</u> forgotten, by us here in the U.S., or by Jesus Himself." ~Mike Spradlin[116]

"Tumaini Ministries provides us a place to make a tangible, measurable difference in another part of our world. Tumaini's work with AIDS orphans and their families is nothing short of amazing, and partnering with them makes more sense than almost anything we have done in the time I have worked at this church. Not only do we support AIDS orphans (350+ currently), but we send teams who assist in a variety of ministry projects. Our eyes and hearts have been opened to needs that we can really do something about, and the results have changed lives in Anaheim as well as in Africa." ~Mike Carman[117]

The Crux of the Matter

Here is the key: God's love. Love for him and for our neighbor. Period. No Christian should ever answer the question, *what could God be saying*, out of guilt. It is a question that can only be answered out of love.

In previous chapters, I introduced the concept of **wa kwetu**, an inclusive idea that the church worldwide is really one. Because we all share the same savior, Holy Spirit and God the father, we are all members of one big family. We know that the essence or the glue that keeps this wa kwetu family together is love. Indeed, without agape love, God's love, there is no way we can treat each other very well. Without agape love, true wa kwetu is not possible. Love then becomes vital in the church's ability to respond to the global calamities around the world, including HIV and AIDS.

Key Bible Passages

Several passages of scripture come to mind when I think of God's love to the forgotten and lost world:

Isaiah 58:1-10 *(NLT)*

"Shout with the voice of the trumpet blast. Shout aloud! Don't be timid. Tell my people Israel of their sins! Yet they act so pious! They come to the Temple every day and seem delighted to learn all about me. They act like a righteous nation that would never abandon the laws of its God. They ask me to take action on their behalf, pretending they want to be near me. 'We have fasted before you', they say. 'Why aren't you impressed?

We have been very hard on ourselves, and you don't even notice it!' 'I will tell you why", I respond. 'It's because you are fasting to please yourselves. Even though you fast, you keep oppressing your workers. What good is fasting if you keep fighting and quarreling? This kind of fasting will never get you anywhere with me. You humble yourselves by going through the motions of penance, bowing your heads like reeds bending in the wind. You dress in burlap and cover yourselves with ashes. Is this what you call fasting? Do you really think this will please the Lord? No, this is the kind of fasting I want: Free those who are wrongly imprisoned; lighten the burden of those who work for you. Let the oppressed go free, and remove the chains that bind people.

Share your food with the hungry, and give shelter to the homeless. Give clothes to those who need them, and do not hide from relatives who need your help. Then your salvation will come like dawn, and your wounds will quickly heal. Your godliness will lead you forward, and the glory of God will protect you from behind. Then when you call the Lord will answer, 'Yes I am here', he will quickly reply. Remove the heavy yoke of oppression. Stop pointing your finger and spreading vicious rumors! Feed the hungry and help those in trouble. Then your light will shine out from the darkness, and the darkness around you will be as bright as noon."

The original recipients of these words were probably the Jews who had returned from captivity. It seems that some of them had a 'holier than thou' attitude. Isaiah minced no words. He challenged them on the difference between true and false worship. He challenged their outward piety and articulated the fasting that really matters to God. Jesus was not impressed with simply external fasting either (see Matthew 6:16; 23:1-39; Luke 18:12). While they fasted, the Jews kept fighting with their neighbors, which is contrary to God's statutes. In the New Testament, Jesus taught that drawing near to God also meant drawing closer to one's neighbor. In fact, love for God and love for neighbor are opposite sides of the same coin as seen in Matthew 22:37-40; John 13:34-35 and I John 1:6-7.

In verse 6 above, Isaiah reminds the people of God that instead of fasting, they should show mercy to those unjustly oppressed. This mercy will be shown by distributing food to the hungry, something that Jesus also taught especially in the story in Matthew 25:6. Verse 10 talks about "light in obscurity". Given the context of this book, this verse is perhaps the most poignant. The essence of the verse is that God's presence is characterized by light. God's presence is represented by his church so when his church focuses on bringing light, such as bringing hope where there is no hope among the AIDS orphans and widows, that is true religion as opposed to simply fasting and taking a 'holier than thou' approach.

Matthew 22:36-40 *(NLT)*

"'Teacher, which is the most important commandment in the Law of Moses?' Jesus replied, 'You must love the Lord your God with all your heart, all your soul and all your mind. This is the first and greatest commandment. A second is equally important: Love your neighbor as yourself. The entire law and

all the demands of the prophets are based on these two commandments'."

When I became a Christian, I 'ate up' every teaching I could put my hands on. I was zealous and wanted to please the Lord in every way and through any means possible. I must admit that in the 1970's, the Pentecostal and charismatic movements had swept East Africa and some of the teachings (particularly on the Holy Sprit) were on the extreme. What I didn't realize until very late in my Christian life was that some of what I did was not really out of my love for God but rather my fear of God. If I missed my Bible study or serious prayer for a day, I felt that I had disappointed God. I had not "shown enough love" that particular day. The truth is, I was afraid of God and wanted to keep him pleased. Little did I realize that I had transferred my poor relationship with my earthly father to my heavenly father. You see, my siblings and I truly feared our father. He was a tough disciplinarian. Most of the time two of my brothers and I we were thoroughly beaten and believe me, on occasion we may have deserved it. But this lifestyle created a big rift between us and our father. We obeyed him because we feared him. It wasn't out of love at all. I feared that I might be struck anytime I didn't meet his standards.

Our heavenly father is completely different from my earthly father. I have been struck by his love, not his rod and that is why I love to serve the poor. He loves us not because of who we are but because it is his nature to love. I am still growing in my love for God though I cannot say that I fully understand how or why he chose to love me. Actually, for me, it is the mystery of not fully understanding God's love that draws me closer to him and the people that he loves, particularly, the people on the fringes of life. In this passage he calls us to love him. We cannot say enough of how incredible it is for God to send his only begotten son to die on our behalf. If we fathom even half of what that statement means, it will make it easier for us to love our neighbors. We know from the story of the Good Samaritan that our neighbor is not necessarily the person next to our property. It can be someone next door or even on the next continent.

Matthew 25:31-40 *(NLT)*

"But when the Son of Man comes in His glory, and all the angels with Him, then He will sit in His glorious throne. All the nations will be gathered in His presence and he will separate the people as the shepherd separates sheep from the goats. And he will place the sheep at his right hand and the goats at his left. Then the King will say to those who are on his right, 'Come, you are blessed by my Father, inherit the Kingdom prepared for you from the creation of the world. For I was hungry and you fed me. I was thirsty, and you gave me a drink. I was a stranger, and you invited me into your home. I was naked, and you gave me clothing. I was sick and you cared for me. I was in prison, and you visited me. Then these righteous ones will say, 'Lord when did we ever see you hungry and feed you? Or thirsty and give you something to drink? Or a stranger and show you hospitality? Or naked and give you clothing? When did we ever see you sick or in prison and visit you? And the King will say, 'I tell you the truth, 'when you did to one of the least of these my brothers and sisters, you were doing it to me!'"

Jesus used this story to paint the picture of the final judgment. The hungry, the thirsty, the stranger, the naked, the sick, and the imprisoned all represent the poor or people in need. Isn't it incredible to think that when we give to the poor, we are actually giving to Jesus himself! We must be careful when we read and apply this passage so that we differentiate between salvation and deeds. Jesus is not saying that we will be saved because we helped the poor. The Bible is abundantly clear that we are saved by grace alone and not by works. Works are important for they give legs to our faith. James put it best, *"How can you show me your faith if you don't have good deeds? I will show you my faith by my good deeds."* Js. 2:18b *(NLT)*.

Compassion, not *pity* was on Jesus' mind during his earthly ministry, all the way to the cross. Twelve times in the New Testament, the Bible records that Jesus was *'moved with compassion,'* each time in the context of his personal confrontation with suffering people.[118] It is instructive to note how the people whom Jesus had compassion on are described. They are the poor, the blind, the crippled, the leprous, the hungry, those who weep, the sick, the little ones, the widows, the captives, those who are weary and heavily burdened with religious legalism, the lost sheep. Clearly Jesus was concerned with the people on the fringes of the society. Shouldn't we?

2 Corinthians 8:1-9 *(NLT)*

> *"Now I want you to know, dear brothers and sisters, what God in His kindness has done through the churches in Macedonia, they are being tested in many troubles, and they are very poor. But they are also filled with abundant joy, which has overflowed in rich generosity. For I can testify that they gave not only what they could afford, but far more. And they did it of their own free will. They begged us again and again for the privilege of sharing in the gift for the believers in Jerusalem.*
>
> *They even did more than we had hoped, for their first action was to give of themselves to the Lord and to us, just as God wanted them to do. So we have urged Titus, who encouraged your giving in the first place, to return to you to finish this ministry of giving. Since you excel in so many ways—in your faith, gifted speakers, your knowledge, your enthusiasm, and your love for us—I want you to also excel in this gracious act of giving. I am not commanding you to do this. But I am testing how genuine your love is by comparing it with the eagerness of other churches.*
>
> *You know the generous grace of our Lord Jesus Christ. Though he was rich, yet for your sakes he became poor, so that by his poverty he could make you rich."*

Here, Paul is talking about the spiritual grace of giving. If you are like me, sometimes you get caught up in wanting to give generously while at the same time being afraid that, given the fluidity of the economy, you may end up in economic ruin yourself. I think for churches, the fear is that giving to outside works will draw funds off from their local needs. This fear is, of course, unfounded. As the text says in vs. 7…giving is a grace that needs to be exercised and to become an excellent part of a believers' spiritual life.

I remember a conversation I had with Pastor Roger.[119] At the time he was pastoring a mega church in Southern California. He said that he had come to believe that people give out of different "buckets". He explained: "…*one is the general fund/Tithe giving…another "bucket" is emerging needs, emergencies, along with two or three other major giving causes.*" Roger went on to share a couple examples to illustrate how this idea of 'buckets' worked for him as a pastor. "*We also had special offerings…one time giving to such crises as the Tsunami, and (Hurricane) Katrina. The Katrina offering was incredible…without prior notification, just an opportunity to give at the close of our weekend services…more than $30,000 was given. The general fund did not suffer a bit…and by allowing such an opportunity, the people learned that generous giving was a pleasure that produces joy in the church.*"

When God's Love Compels Us

In his breathtaking book, *Crazy Love,* Pastor Francis Chan shares a personal touching testimony. "…*when I returned from my first trip to Africa, I felt very strongly that we were to sell our house and move into something smaller, in order to give more away. The feedback I got was along the lines of, 'It's not fair to your kids,' 'Its not a prudent financial choice,' and 'You are doing it just for show.' I do not remember a single person who encouraged me to explore it or supported the decision at that time.*"[120] Reading the reaction to Francis's bold move didn't surprise me at all. When my wife and I decided to give a share of our property in Kenya to build a multi-purpose community center for AIDS orphans and the community, we got a similar response. Not from non-believers but from the local Christian community. Some said, 'They must have received money from Americans as compensation,' or, 'Nobody gives two acres of prime land in Kenya for free.' I do not remember one person encouraging us to go ahead with the decision at the time. The fact is, we cannot out-give God. I agree with Chan that to love God with all we have is crazy and will not always make sense to our closest friends, including Christians. We need to do it anyway. I was really challenged to read the decision that Pastor Chan and his leadership at *Cornerstone Community Church* in Simi Valley, California made on giving. They took what some would consider a radical move with respect to giving more to the poor. In 2008, they committed to give away 50 percent of their budget because they *"believe that when Jesus said to "love your neighbor as yourself" He wasn't kidding".*[121]

They went further and made another radical decision to scale down on their building budget. *"Initially, we had a beautiful plan for a new sanctuary that would have cost many millions of dollars. Now, however, we are in the process of getting permits to build an outdoor amphitheater that will seat plenty of people and save us about $20 million. I am sure there will be days when it's uncomfortable outside, but there will also be joy in knowing that we're sitting in the cold so that someone else can have a blanket.*[122]

Wow! What love for God and neighbor! And Finally, There's Joe

I want to leave you with the story of an encounter I had several months ago with a man in a Southern California town. I will call him "Joe". Of the many encounters I have had with donors, I will never forget this unplanned meeting with Joe. I had just finished talking about the work I do in Africa with the AIDS orphans and widows. As I normally do, I had concluded my presentation with a question, what could God be saying to you in response? Out in the lobby, I found several people waiting to greet me. Some were friends and acquaintances that I had met and known over the years. I looked down the line and my eyes came into contact with Joe's. I don't know why or how but somehow I could tell he was anxious to meet and to talk to me. When I finally made my way to where Joe was standing, he shook my hand warmly and with a big smile proceeded to hug me tightly. As we began to talk, he got very emotional as he poured out what was on his heart. Here is gist what he had to say:

"Stanley, I liked what you shared about your work with the AIDS population in Africa. I applaud you for the work you do and wish there were more people like you responding to the needs of children in Africa. I hate to see the faces of those innocent babies who are born to AIDS patients and what awaits them. I hate to hear the stories of those teenagers growing up without parents. It grieves my heart to hear about grandmothers who have become mothers again. I am so sorry Stanley because I have no money to give you. I do not even have a bank account—it is a long story- but I have $20.00 which I want to split with you guys. I have no job. In fact, I am homeless. I do however have something I feel the Lord tugging my heart that I want to give you. I want to give you my AIDS medicine to help someone dying of AIDS in Africa. They probably need it more than I do."

At this point I was also getting emotional myself. I knew I should not waste that divine moment. I knew that God wanted to remind me an important lesson in my service to him. All God's people matter to him and they should all matter to me. Here was an ordinary Christian man—or was he ordinary? Joe was genuinely touched by the sufferings of innocent babies, teenagers who grew up with no parents and grandmothers who had become parents all over again due to AIDS. Here was an ordinary Christian who was genuinely exhibiting what should be the response of Christians all over the world when we learn of the challenges facing our brothers and sisters –may that be war, hunger, persecution or AIDS. Or does Joe understand the impact of AIDS better because he is a sufferer himself? But as Bob Pierce prayed many years, shouldn't all Christians be touched by the things that touch the heart of God? In Joe I saw an ordinary Christian demonstrating how global Christians who understand **wa kwetu**, that we are all in this together, should respond to the sufferings around the globe. Here was an ordinary Christian, a man at the bottom of the economic barrel, who responded to God's call with what he had in hand. Not just what he had in hand but with the only thing of value that he owned, $10.00 and his AIDS medicines. Indeed, by offering to give away his lifeline medicine, he was offering his very life!

What could God be saying to you today?

ENDNOTES

Forward

[1] Foster, G., *Study of the Responseby Faith-Based Organizations to Orphans and Vulnerable Children*. Study commissioned by World Conference of Religions for Peace and United Nations Children Fund, 2001.

[2] Mutunga provides the meaning of the Kiswahili phrase, "Wa kwetu means 'one who is from my home,' or 'one from my family'.

Chapter One

[1] Kenya National AIDS Control Council, 2007; UNAIDS & World Health Organization, 2007.

[2] Kenya National AIDS Control Council, 2007.

[3] Joint Report by UNAIDS & World Health Organization, 2007.

[4] The Problem with Pain, 1962.

Chapter Two

[5] At the Millennium Summit in September 2000 the largest gathering of world leaders in history adopted the UN Millennium Declaration, committing their nations to a new global partnership to reduce extreme poverty and setting out a series of time-bound targets, with a deadline of 2015 that have become known as the Millennium Development Goals.

[6] *Hunger Isn't History* in Christianity Today, November 2008:26-33.

[7] *The Whiteman's Burden: Why the West's Efforts to Aid the Rest Have Done so much Ill and So Little Good*, New York: The Penguin Press, 2006, Pages 5-6.

[8] Easterly, p.6.

[9] Nov. 3rd, 2008 World Bank Updates Poverty Estimates for the Developing World.

[10] *Africa Unchained: The Blueprint for Africa's Future*. New York: Palgrave MacMillan, 2005. Page23.

[11] See an excellent article, *Why aid-addicted Africa remains in deep poverty*, in The Wall Street Journal: Business Daily, January 1, 2009: 16-17

[12] *The Bottom Billion: Why the Poorest Countries Are Failing and What Can Be Done About it*. Paul Collier. London: Oxford University Pres, 2007, page 5.

[13] Ibid. page 7.

[14] This is according to *Kenya Vision 2030*, page ix., 2008 Edition.

[15] *Africa Unchained: The Blueprint for Africa's Future*. New York:Palgrave MacMillan, 2005. Page2

[16] Financial Times, July 9, 2003; page 1.

[17] Ministry of State for Planning National Development and Vision 2030.

[18] *Daily Nation*, June 7th, 2009—by Peter Orengo.

[19] Ibid.

[20] *East African Standard*, July 2nd, 2009—Lucianne Limo Jeremiah Kiplangat & Job Ogonga.

[21] Ibid

[22] The East African Standard, July 10th, 2009

[23] Ibid

[24] A Suffi story told by Sister Joan Chittister, a Benedictine nun – quoted in *The Language of God* , by Francis S. Collins, page 26.

[25] See his book, Creating A World Without Poverty, 2007, pg 12.

Chapter Three

[26] www.crin.org

[27] You can read more of the changing world view in my previous work, *"Who Raises the Child When There is No Village"* a book chapter in <u>Footprints of God</u> edited by Charles Van Engen, Nancy Thomas and Robert Gallagher, MARC, World Vision, 1999

[28] I have explained extensively this concept in my earlier work, *"Toward Wa Kwetu Without Strangers"* in <u>Tribalism and Ethnicity,</u> 1997, pages 9-84.

[29] See Above.

[30] See above.

[31] See <u>African Religions and Philosophy</u>, 1969, page 108.

[32] For more details see his <u>Corporate Personality in Traditional Igbo Society and the Sacrament of Reconciliation,</u> 1995:xxl.

[33] Paul G. Hiebert in <u>The Gospel in Human Contexts</u>, 2009, page135 argues that Western cultures have predominantly a mechanistic world view while most of the developing world has an organic worldview??

[34] See his book, Anthropological Insights for Missionaries:

[35] Larretta Schrader sharing her experience after a Vision Trip to see her kids in Kenya

[36] *New Dictionary of Theology*. Edited by Clair Ferguson and David Wright. Intervarsity Press. 1988, pages 251-252.

[37] In December 2007, there was a general election in Kenya to elect the President, members of parliament and municipal councilors. The Presidential elections proved to be very acrimonious. Under very suspicious circumstances, the incumbent was declared winner but another major candidate also claimed victory. A tribal war of sorts ensued through January 2008 and many innocent lives were lost. Through the intervention of the international community, a compromise was reached between the two principals and a coalition government was formed

Chapter Four

[38] "Chokora" is a Kiswahili derogative term, historically used on urban street children. These children are known for their anti-social behaviors and are considered an eye soar and a nuisance to the society. It is therefore a very hurtful insult even to the street children let alone some innocent victim of poverty circumstances such as Grace.

[39] Worden, page 14.

[40] Ibid 14,15.

[41] Ibid 16.

[42] Ibid 27.

[43] Parenting Through Crisis: Helping Kids in Times of Loss, Grief, and Change. Barbara Coloroso. New York: Harper Resource, 2000.

[44] Ibid. 26-27.

[45] In the local Kikamba language, Nga Musyoki means, one who always returns.

Chapter Five

[46] Engaging People in Sustainability. D Tillbury and D. Wortman, 2004

[47] Education and Development: Measuring the Social Benefits. London: Oxford University, 2002

[48] Literature Review on the Impact of Education Levels on HIV/AIDS Prevalence Rates, WFP, March, 2006.

Chapter Six

[49] CS Lewis, The Problem with Pain, 1962.

[50] The Dance of Life: Weaving Sorrows And Blessings into One Joyful Step Henri J. Nouwen and Michael Ford, 2006.

[51] Mike Goldsworthy is the Lead Pastor at Parkcrest Christian Church in Long Beach, California.

[52] July 20, 2009, *40 years later, moon landing is still giant leap for mankind*, in Honolulu Advertiser.com.

[53] "Africa's missing billions: International arms flows and cost of conflict". August 2007, in IANSA.

[54] Ibid.

[55] Ibid

[56] World Bank report, 2008.

[57] Ibid

[58] U.N report by Director-General Jacques Diouf on June 19th, 2009.

[59] Ibid

[60] Ibid

[61] For details read his book, The Bottom Billion: Why the Poorest Countries Are Falling and What Can Be Done About It, London: Oxford University Press, 2007.

[62] Collier, pages 6, 7.

[63] Collier, page 7

[64] For a thorough discussion on this important topic, read A Farewell to Alms: A Brief Economic History of the World. Princeton: Princeton University Press, 2007, page 3.

[65] Ibid, 3

[66] UNICEF Report, *Progress for Children*, September 30, 2005.

[67] William Easterly, The Whiteman's Burden: Why the West's Efforts to aid the Rest have done so much ill and so little good, 2006, page 4

[68] Jeffrey Sachs, The End of Poverty: Economic Possibilities for Our Time, 2005.

[69] President's Quarterly Report, April, 2009

Chapter Seven

[70] The Gospel in Human Contexts: Anthropological Explorations for Contemporary Missions. Grand Rapids: Baker Academic, 2009, pages 194-96

[71] Ibid, 194-96.

[72] Ibid, 194-96

[73] Anthropology for Christian Witness. Maryknoll: Orbis Books, 1999. pages 440-41.

Chapter Eight

[74] Pages 123-126

[75] For details, see Glenn J. Schwartz, When Charity Destroys Dignity: Overcoming Unhealthy Dependency in the Christian Movement. Lancaster, PA: World Mission Associate, 2007. PP 251-252.

[76] "Teen Missions being Retooled" by Neil in <u>Washington Post</u>, July 31, 2008.

[77] Neil.

[78] Walking with the Poor: Principles and Practices of Transformational Development. New York: Orbis Books, 2000. pgs 115-119.

Chapter Nine

[79] For a detailed description of HEART's work, visit their website: www.africaheart.com

[80] I discussed the impact of this event in chapter 7. *Vijana Tusemesane* means, *"Youths, let's gather together and reason out" taken from Isa.1:18.* The group meets every Saturday. This is a forum where all kinds of challenges are addressed openly. At such a meeting in spring 2009, a gun was turned in to the leaders after a discussion on drugs and social ills that lead youths to commit murders in the slums.

[81] A detailed analysis of this development theory is discussed in Kretzmann & McKnight's book, Building Societies from Inside Out, 1993

[82] Ibid, pages 346-354

[83] David Cooperrider L. and Suresh Srivastva. 1987. *Appreciative Inquiry in Organizational Life*, in Research in Organizational Change and Development 1, 129-69.

[84] David Cooperrider L., Jim Ludema, Suresh Srivastva, and Craig Wishart. 1995. Appreciative Inquiry: A Constructuve Approach to Organizational Capacity Building ,". A Workshop for World Vision Relief and Development . Department of Organizational Behavior , Wetherhead School of Management, Case Western Reserve, Cleveland, Ohio (May)

[85] Bryant Myers, Walking with The Poor: Principles and Practices of Transformational Development. Maryknoll, NY: Orbis Books, 2000. Page 175.

[86] Johnson and Laudema 1997, page 75

Chapter Ten

[87] Dr. Ron Jurgensen is the proprietor of Ronald Jurgensen Dental Inc, Newport Beach, California. He has made several vision trips to Africa, the latest in spring 2009.

[88] Lonny Myers is the Executive Director of Joshua International Medical Group, Buena Park, California. This report was compiled after the team's vision trip in summer 2009.

[89] Adapted from The Star Thrower by Loren Eiseley (1907 – 1977)

[90] The Millennium Development Goals (MDGs) are eight goals to be achieved by 2015 that respond to the world's main development challenges. The MDGs were drawn from the actions and targets contained in the **Millennium Declaration** that was adopted by 189 nations-and signed by 147 heads of state and governments during the UN Millennium Summit in September 2000.

[91] www.UNICEF.org, 2007 Report on world immunization

[92] World Health Organization: World Malaria Report 2008. "WHO / HIM / GMP / 2008 / 1"

[93] For example, there is no agreement among scholars whether or not Jesus went to Matthew's house immediate after his call or much later. Also, although Matthew indicates that Jesus went to Jairus' house immediately after visiting him (9:18), both Mark (5:21) and Luke (8:40) indicate that, such a visit was at much later period after Jesus' return from the country of Gardarenes.

Chapter Eleven

[94] Laretta Shrader is the Missions Pastor at First Christian Church, Yuma, AZ

[95] According to Lausanne Statistical Task Force, 1999 there is one believer for every 9 non believers.

[96] For example, according to David B. Barrett in World Christian Encyclopedia 2001, the non-White indigenous church increased eleven-fold to 11% of all Christians by 1996. See also Barrett, "Status of Global Mission", IBMR, 1996.

[97] A Study on Major Religions of the World. Last edited in August 2007. See also David B. Barrett's 2001 edition of the *World Christian Encyclopedia* stated there were 2.1 billion Christians in the world, or 33% of the total population

[98] See, for example, Ralph Winter and Bruce Koch's detailed analysis in Perspectives on the World Christian Movement, 1999.

[99] See Barrett and Johnson in Our Globe, 1990. Bryant Myers in The Poor and the Lost, 1989, makes the same point

[100] Reverend Jesse Jackson in eulogy for Ennis Crosby

[101] *Christopher Murray, M.D., Ph.D., Director of WHO's Global Programmed on Evidence for Health Policy, 2000*

[102] WHO: 50 Facts on World Health Report, 2009.

[103] Walking with the Poor, New York: Orbits Books. 2000, page 49.

Chapter Twelve

[104] Vickie is a colleague in ministry and the Founder and President of HEART—Health Education Africa Resource Teams. They are based in Nairobi and work in the slums with AIDS orphans and HIV positive widows.

[105] TAA stands for Tumaini Alumni Alliance

[106] World Bank's definition in Bamberger and Cheema, 1990.

[107] U.S. Agency for International Development, 1988.

[108] www.ithaca.edu./sustainability files: Sustainable Measures, 2002.

[109] www.ithaca.edu/sustainability files. Emphasis added.

[110] Walking with the Poor: Principles and Practices of Transformational Development, pages 128-133.

Chapter Thirteen

[111] Mike Goldsworthy is the Lead Pastor, Parkcrest Christian Church, and Long Beach, California.

[112] Kerry Decker is the Senior Pastor, Pathway Christian Church, Riverside, California.

[113] Laretta Schrader is the Missions Pastor at First Christian Church in Yuma, Arizona.

[114] Mike Spradlin is the Senior Pastor, Valley Christian Church, Chino, California.

[115] Mike Carman is the Cross Cultural Ministries Pastor at Knott Avenue Christian Church, Anaheim, California

[116] Matthew 9:36; 14:14; 15:32; 18:27; 20:34; Mark 1:41;6:34; 8:2;9:22; Luke 7:13; 10:33; 15:20.

[117] Until his retirement in June 2008, Dr. Roger Beard was the Lead pastor at Parkcrest Christian Church in Long Beach California. He had pastured there for 38 years.

[118] For details, read Crazy Love: Overwhelmed by a Relentless God. Francis Chan and Danae Yankoski. Colorado Springs, CO: David C. Cook, 2008, pages 135-136.

[119] Ibid, page 163.

[120] Ibid, page 163.

Stanley M. Mutunga

References Cited

Attey, George. Africa Unchained: The Blueprint for Africa's Future. New York: Palgrave MacMillan, 2005.

Bamberger, Michael and Shabbir Cheema, World Bank's definition of sustainability , 1990.

Barrett, David "Annual Statistical Table on Global Mission", 1995, IBMR;

Barrett, David, "Status of Global Mission", IBMR, 1996.

Barrett, David and Todd Johnson in Our Globe and How to Reach It, Birmingham, Al: Woman's Missionary Union Publishers, 1990.

Chan, Francis and Danae Yankoshi. Crazy Love: Overwhelmed By a Relentless God. Colorado Springs, CO: David C. Cook, 2008.

Clark, Gregory A Farewell to Alms: A Brief Economic History of the World. Princeton: Princeton University Press, 2007.

Collier, Paul. The Bottom Billion: Why the Poorest Countries Are Failing and What Can Be Done About it. London: Oxford University Pres, 2007.

Collins, Francis S. The Language of God: A Scientist Presents Evidence for Belief. New York: Simon & Schuster, 2007.

Coloroso , Barbara Parenting through Crisis: Helping Kids in Times of Loss, Grief, and Change.. New York: Harper Resource, 2000

Cooperrider L., David and Suresh Srivastva. "Appreciative Inquiry in Organizational Life", in Research in Organizational Change and Development 1, 129-69, 1987.

Cooperrider ,David L., Jim Ludema, Suresh Srivastva, and Craig Wishart.. "Appreciative Inquiry: A Constructive Approach to Organizational Capacity Building ,". A Workshop for World Vision Relief and Development . Department of Organizational Behavior, Wetherhead School of Management, Case Western Reserve, Cleveland, Ohio (May). 1995

Daily Nation, June 7th, 2009—by Peter Orengo.

Diouf, Jacques, Director- General U.N report, June 19th, 2009.

Easterly, William. The Whiteman's Burden: Why the West's Efforts to Aid the Rest Have Done so much Ill and So Little Good. New York: The Penguin Press, 2006.

East African Standard, July 2nd, 2009—Lucianne Limo Jeremiah Kiplangat & Job Ogonga.

East African Standard, July 10th, 2009

Echema, Austin Corporate Personality in Traditional Igbo Society and the Sacrament of Reconciliation, 1995:xxl.

Eiseley, Loren. The Star Thrower (1907 – 1977).

Ferguson, Clair and David Wright, (Editors). Chicago: New Dictionary of Theology. Intervarsity Press, 1988.

Financial Times, July 9, 2003.

Ford, Michael and Henri J. M. Nouwen The Dance of Life: Weaving Sorrows and Blessings into One Joyful Step. Maria Press, 2006.

Friedman, Thomas. The World is Flat. Farrar, Straus & Giroux publishers, 2005.

Hernandez, Nelson. *40 years later, moon landing is still giant leap for mankind*, Washington Post quoted in Honolulu Advertiser.com, July 20, 2009.

Hiebert, Paul G. The Gospel in Human Contexts: Anthropological Explorations for Contemporary Missions. Grand Rapids: Baker Academic, 2009.

Hiebert, Paul G. Anthropological Insights for Missionaries. Grand Rapids: Baker Publishing Group, 1986.

International Action Network on Small Arms, Oxfam International and Safer world. "Africa's missing billions: International arms flows and cost of conflict", August 2007

Joint Report by UNAIDS & World Health Organization, 2007.

Johnstone, Patrick, Operation World, 1993.

Kenya, *Ministry of State for Planning National Development: Vision 2030*, 2008.

Kenya, *National AIDS Control Council*, 2007.

Kraft, Charles. Anthropology for Christian Witness. Mary knoll: Orbis Books, 1999.

Kretzmann, John P. and John L. McKnight. Building Societies from Inside Out: A Path Toward Finding and Mobilizing a Community's Assets. Evanston, IL: Northwestern University, 1993.

Koch, Bruce and Ralph Winter. Perspectives on the World Christian Movement, Pasadena, CA, 1999.

Lewis, C.S. The Problem with Pain, 1962

McMahon, Walter W. Education and Development: Measuring the Social Benefits. London: Oxford University, 2002.

Mbiti, John. African Religions and Philosophy. Heinemann (2nd sub edition) 1992.

Morgan, Timothy. "Hunger Isn't History" in Christianity Today, November 2008:26-33.

Mutunga , Stanley M. President's Quarterly Report, Tumaini International Ministries. Brea, CA, April, 2009.

Mutunga , Stanley M., *"Who Raises the Child When There is No Village"* a book chapter in Footprints of God edited by, MARC, World Vision, 1999.Edited by Charles Van Engen, Nancy Thomas and Robert Gallagher.

Mutunga, Stanley M. *"Toward Wa Kwetu Without Strangers"* in Tribalism and Ethnicity, 1997, pages 9-84. Edited by Elie Buchonyori

Murray, Christopher. WHO's Global Program on Evidence for Health Policy, 2000.

Myers, Bryant.Walking with the Poor: Principles and Practices of Transformational Development. New York: Orbis Books, 2000.

Myers, Bryant. The Poor and the Lost. MARC EUROPE, 1988.

Roberts Jr., Bob. Glocalization: How Followers of Jesus Engage..the New Flat World. Grand Rapids: Zondervan, 2007.

Roberts Jr., Bob. Transformation: How Glocal Churches Transform Lives and the World. Grand Rapids: Zondervan, 2006.

Sachs, Jeffrey. The End of Poverty: Economic Possibilities for Our Time. New York: Penguin Press, 2005.

Samura, Sorious. *Why aid-addicted Africa remains in deep poverty*, in The Wall Street Journal: Business Daily, January 1, 2009: 16-17.

Schwartz, Glenn J. When Charity Destroys Dignity: Overcoming Unhealthy Dependency in the Christian Movement. Lancaster, PA: World Mission Associate, 2007.

Teen Missions being Retooled. Neil in Washington Post, July 31, 2008.

Tillbury,Daniella and David Wortman. *Engaging People in Sustainability: World Bank,.2004.*

Worden, J. William. Children and Grief: When a Parent Dies. The Guilford Press, 1996.

WWW: *Children Rights Information Network.org*

WWW.ithaca.edu./sustainability files: Sustainable Measures, 2002.

WWW: UNICEF: *Report on world immunization, 2007.*

WWW: UNICEF: *Report on* Progress *for Children,* September 30, 2005.

WWW: United Nations: *Millennium Declaration, for 2015*, September 2000.

WWW: World Bank: *Poverty Estimates for the Developing World*, Nov. 3rd, 2008.

WWW: World Food Program: *The Impact of Education Levels on HIV/AIDS Prevalence Rates in Africa*, March, 2006.

WWW: World Health Organization: *50 Facts on World Health Report*, 2009.

WWW: World Health Organization: *World Report on Malaria, WHO/HIM/GMP/2008/1*.

Yunus, Muhammad. Creating a World without Poverty: Social Business and the Future of Capitalism. Public Affairs publishers, 2008.

Additional Information

To learn more about the three ministries covered in this book, you can visit their respective websites as follows:

Tumaini international Ministries www:Tumainiinternational.org

Health Education Africa Resource Teams (HEART): www.africaheart.com

Community Transformers: Information about this ministry available at www.africaheart.com

Stanley M. Mutunga

Stanley Mutunga is available for speaking engagements and personal appearances. For more information contact:

Stanley Mutunga
C/O Advantage Books
P.O. Box 160847
Altamonte Springs, Florida 32716

To purchase additional copies of this book or other books published by Advantage Books call our toll free order number at:
1-888-383-3110 (Book Orders Only)

or visit our bookstore website at:
www.advbookstore.com

Longwood, Florida, USA
"we bring dreams to life"™
www.advbooks.com

Stanley M. Mutunga